YOU CAN'T
YELL IT!

Dora:
To a sweet lady
and a great friend —
Best wishes
Bill Poston
24 Feb 2016

COMING OF AGE IN LEEDS, IOWA

WILLIAM K. POSTON JR.

outskirtspress

DENVER, COLORADO

You Can Yell It!
Coming of Age in Leeds, Iowa
All Rights Reserved.
Copyright © 2016 William K. Poston Jr.
V6.0

Outskirts Press, Inc.
http://www.outskirtspress.com

ISBN: 978-1-4787-6669-8

Outskirts Press and the "OP" logo are trademarks belonging to Outskirts Press, Inc.

PRINTED IN THE UNITED STATES OF AMERICA

Leeds High School, 1939-1972 Leeds, Iowa

The older some people get, the more they want to talk about their past. (Dr. John Miller, 2013)

Table of Contents

Preface:
Leeds – Some things you never forget

Here I sit, nearly sixty years after graduating from Leeds High School, and the tune and words of our venerable school song still reverberate through my mind:

LEEDS HIGH SCHOOL SONG (Sung to the tune of *On Wisconsin*)

You can yell it, you can spell it – *L-E-E-D-S!*
Skies are clear, the foe is here, it's time to do your best — L-H-S!
Do or die, we're feeling high, so let your colors fly
There's the goal, come on let's go — for old Leeds High! Fight!

What is it about a place that embeds its memories so strongly in our consciousness? To people that passed through on their way to some-where else, Leeds was not noteworthy or remarkable. It was just a blue-collar neighborhood area northeast of Sioux City along the "Blue Star Highway" (US Highway 75 — north on Floyd Avenue under and past the viaduct). Going south on 75 would take you to Dallas, Texas (and on to Galveston), and going north would take you through West Fargo, North Dakota and on to Noyes, Minnesota on the Canadian border. In my limited world, north-bound on Highway 75 would get you to Hinton, Wren,[1] Merrill, and LeMars (home of Blue Bunny ice cream!). With a slight change in direction in northern Iowa, you could

---

[1] Wren wasn't actually a town, but it was a railroad stop for some reason – probably to get water for steam locomotives. It was characterized by a sign alongside the railroad tracks on the east side of Highway 75. Only one house was visible in the vicinity of the sign, located midway between Leeds and LeMars.

even get to the magical Twin Cities. [2]

But to those of us that lived there, it was a wonderland of experiences, good and not so good, but remembered with deep and long-lasting fondness and affection. At least that's true for me. I feel blessed to have grown up in Leeds during the mid-20th Century – before, during, and after two wars, the nuclear age, and the fertile social, economic, and natural environment – which encourages me to share my thoughts and memories with others.

Sioux City Postcard (c. 1940)[3]

This book is not intended to be only about me, but it's meant to be a collection of memories of a time in the mid-twentieth century in northwestern Iowa – random and nostalgic reminiscences of a boy who grew up in Leeds, attended school from kindergarten through

---

[2] The twin cities of Minneapolis and St. Paul were the epitome of civilization in the upper Midwest, and full of wonder for small town kids like me. My first visit in 1948 took me to the top of the Foshay Tower, which nearly took my breath away due to its height of over 400 feet. Decades later, it's tough to find the Tower among the giant skyscrapers of the Minneapolis skyline.

[3] Starting at top left clockwise, this collector card shows the Woodbury County Courthouse, the Sioux City Auditorium, the downtown Sioux City Post Office, the Grandview Park Band Shell, and the Memorial Cemetery Bell Tower in Morningside.

high school there, benefited from many relationships with amazing people, enjoyed an abundance of extraordinary escapades, and who left for more adventurous places and exciting activities (or so I imagined), around the world.

Of course, I often speculate about the accuracy of my memory after so many years. One blessing I had was that my Mother was half-Irish, Catholic, and from a large family. I spent multitudinous hours listening to my Irish relatives narrating wonderful stories. I learned that a good story was not always enhanced by a rigorous adherence to veracity, but I'll do the best I can to achieve accuracy. Amazingly, memories of Leeds, some fuzzy but genuine, have continued to warm my heart and tickle my funny bone at times in the nearly six decades since. Why was Leeds so special? I think I have some truths about that, which are worth sharing.

I heard an author once say that truths are like a pizza party. Several of us may enjoy the same pizza, but with different pieces. Each piece is unique, and is influenced by our human limitations of perception. I aim to share my perceptions, as correctly as possible, but I know that others may have a different piece of perception about life in Leeds. In any case, I focused on the question, "what was the quality and character of Leeds?" More importantly, what was its impact on my youth and others' childhood? My impressions of possible answers arise from what follows.

A personal note about this book. The book is written in the first person to create simple and straightforward conversation without pretense. By and large it is a personal memoir and reminiscent of times long gone by. It is intended to serve no purpose in glorifying my life or my work. After writing well over a dozen books within my profession, this book erupted for pure enjoyment as I reflected and ruminated about my youth, the friends and family that helped shape my life and future, and a place along a river in Iowa that I genuinely still hold close to my heart.[4]

Though it is many decades later, Leeds still enriches my spirit and I wish these memories – factual or unintentionally embellished by time or the limitations of memory – to be freely given in a manifestation of love for my children, grandchildren and their children yet to come and my extended family and friends

---

[4] Memories are shared with an intention to achieve accuracy, but one has to be reminded that I am part Irish, I've kissed the Blarney Stone in Ireland, so as my Mother used to say, accuracy and truth should not get in the way of a good story. My version may be amiss due to the many years that have passed by, but I compose it with a smile and occasional chuckle. I hope you find it amusing too.

I.

The Leeds Setting: A small town (almost) within a larger city

"The poetry of the earth is never dead."   — <u>John Keats</u>

After I was grown and out on my own in distant places, I was occasionally asked where I was from or where I grew up. I sometimes felt challenged with what seemed to be a minor conundrum. Depending upon who asked and where we were at the time might cause me to respond sort of generally, "I'm from the Midwestern United States." If asked as to which state, I would respond, "Iowa," but if pressed for more specificity, I often would say with an attempt at humor, "near Sioux City, which is on the west coast of the state of Iowa" (Missouri River). If they persisted, I might then say, "Well, I'm really from Leeds." Such specificity demanded the interrogatories, because if I had initially given "Leeds" as my response, it would be met with a blank look and the inevitable follow up: "Where's that?"

Of course, most people didn't know where Leeds was and they usually didn't seem interested in learning more than that. But those of us from Leeds never minded the disinterested response, because <u>we</u> knew where it was. And we knew that during the 1940's and 1950's, we had grown up in a special unique little world – really a small town, at the time about three miles outside of Sioux City. Some realized that Leeds, which had been an independent town in the country actually was annexed by Sioux City in 1891. After that, it was within the Sioux City limits, but to those of us who lived in Leeds; our small town was worlds apart – self-contained, independent, and culturally unique. Sioux City almost seemed like another place.

In fact, Leeds was a place not only with singular qualities, but it was one of those rare places with character melded from dynamics derived from its geography, societal distinctiveness, wide-ranging spirituality, and socioeconomic diversity. Every now and then, I often remember and reflect upon my growing up years in Leeds with astonishing nostalgia – often rising to euphoric levels – especially if I'm with my favorite childhood buddy – Bob Harward. Bob and I agree that it's really hard to come up with any negative feelings when we think about our time in Leeds.

Leeds was apparently named after its British counterpart in County Kent, England. I learned in school that the City of Leeds has a magnificent castle, and it made me feel like I was somehow associated with royalty.

Leeds Castle, Kent, England

While I grew up in Leeds, I didn't quite manage to be born there. Something less than spectacular occurred at St. Joseph's Hospital on 21st and Court Streets, Sioux City, Iowa, on November 11, 1938 at 2:30 in the morning, when I came into this world. At the time I was born, my Dad, Ken Poston[5] was employed as a truck driver out of Beresford, South Dakota, about 50 miles from Sioux City. He hauled beef from the Sioux City meat packing companies[6] to the Black Hills area. At that time, he was making $12 a week, but after I was born, his boss gave him a $3 raise. That's the least expensive value ever put on my precious soul to this day that I know of. But it was a handsome sum in those days. In fact, I learned that prices were comparatively low enough to fit into those wages. Some sample prices:[7]

Milk was 50¢/gallon
Loaf of bread was 9¢
A new car (Ford Deluxe Coupe) was $685
Gas was 10¢/gallon
Hamburger was 13¢/pound
Average annual wages per year were $1730 (Dad made about $750/year)
The Dow Jones average on the New York Stock Exchange was $154.76!

Nevertheless, it's relevant in that at the age of 18 months, we moved into Leeds – in a very modest home commensurate with our economic standing — which began my fascination with Leeds history, characteristics, demographics, and activities.

---

[5] My Dad's name was William Kenneth Poston, but he went by Ken. He was called Billy in his early life, but preferred his middle name later. Of course, I was named after him, and I will share a wrinkle or two about fun that sometimes caused.
[6] Sioux City was an important meat processing city, with a very large stockyards and a number of packing plants, including Swift's, Armour's, and Cudahy's.
[7] Adapted from http://www.answers.com/Q/What_did_things_cost_in_1938.

It was a separate and special place – unlike anywhere else I've been. For example, we had our own school system in Leeds with two schools—Hawthorne Elementary, built 1892, for grades K-6, and Leeds High School, built 1939, for grades 7-12). Officially the two Leeds schools were part of the Sioux City Schools, but that was over our horizon and didn't seem relevant to our lives and activities, except maybe at graduation when some school board members and administrative dignitaries would come and deliver uplifting, and immediately forgettable, speeches. Regrettably, both schools are closed now, with Hawthorne standing mute and unoccupied after 122 years, and Leeds High School torn down.[8] A new elementary school sits on its old site on Jefferson Street.

Floyd Avenue, Leeds, Iowa 1911

---

[8] Leeds High School's life span was only 33 years as a high school, when in 1972, it was converted first to a junior high school and later into a Kindergarten-Grade 3 primary school in the Sioux City Community School System. Leeds students were moved to North High School. Leeds High was demolished in 2010, giving the building that we all thought was indestructible only 71 years of longevity. I have a brick salvaged from the old school on my desk to keep its memory alive.

Even many decades after being annexed by Sioux City, Leeds continued to operate as a separate entity. Moving up and down Floyd Avenue, it was easy to spot our own fire station that said "Leeds" on the fascia of the building, a bank that said "Leeds Bank" on the building front, Wilkins Rexall drug store, Leeds' Bakery – a full service bakery with savory Bismarcks (jelly-filled, vanilla-frosted pastries), a beauty parlor, a hardware store, a "variety" store, a lodge hall above the bakery, Burke's Lumber Yard (that sold coal), two very independently unique barbers (Shorty Girard and Jim Primm), three – count them, three – gas stations (Wixon's Conoco, Stesse's Standard, and Pettit's Sinclair) and five grocery stores, one of which was a general store – Siedschlag's – with just about everything in it – groceries, meat, clothing, shoes, hardware, appliances, you name it. The Leeds Tavern was at the north end of the business section and attracted a fair number of customers, including my Dad, who usually stopped in for a beer and some chin wagging with his buddies after work.

Amazingly, the fact that Leeds actually had <u>five</u> grocery stores that served a population of something less than 2300 residents[9] was puzzling. Our family had dealings with all five of the stores from time to time and most of us knew the owners personally. Harry Siedschlag owned Siedschlag's General Store and lived down the block from our home on Central Avenue,[10] Cliff Watt, father of another buddy now

---

[9] The population of 2300 is an estimate. However, Leeds' population was included in the 1950 census of Sioux City with 83991 residents. The Leeds population was estimated by using the population per square mile of Sioux City (1436) and multiplying it by Leeds square mileage (1.586) giving Leeds an estimated population of 2277 (rounded up to 2300). Any estimate could be more – it could be less – but it still qualifies as a small town despite being part of Sioux City, especially since Leeds was three miles away at the time.

[10] Our street had several landmark homes and buildings – some prominent merchants' homes, Hawthorne Elementary School, the Methodist and Lutheran churches – and we lived at the top of the hill where the concrete paving ended at 46th Street in front of our house. 46th Street on our north side and Central extending farther north were clay – hard as a rock when dry but like soupy quicksand when wet. To dig when wet required a sump pump but when dry a jack hammer.

deceased – Dick Watt – owned Watts Grocery, Lee Kuhn owned Lee's IGA Super Market, Clair Benton owned Brown's Fine Foods, and the Council Oak Grocery was part of a small regional grocery chain. The Council Oak was named after a tree high up on Prospect Hill – one of the chain of loess hills above the Missouri River where Lewis and Clark had met with the local Sioux Indians about 150 years before when the expedition was trying to find a waterway to the Pacific coast.

Council Oak Foods on Leeds Main Street 1952

In addition to those five grocery stores, Mr. and Mrs. Garvey had a little neighborhood store in the front of their house on the southeast corner of 45th and Polk Streets – something that now might be considered a convenience market – albeit rather small and Spartan in its existence, but containing several staples. The store was literally in the front of their house; the Garveys lived in the back.

I didn't realize it at the time, but I think now that the Garveys may have unintentionally and unknowingly originated perhaps the earliest version of the neighborhood convenience market – now ubiquitous all over the country almost on every corner (e.g., Casey's, Kum & Go, Quik Trip, 7-11, etc.). Lacking sufficient foresight, that opportunity escaped my career path. However, their little store (and I mean little) did provide sustenance to our family from time to time. Once in a while, Mom would be making bologna (we pronounced it 'baloney') spread[11] only to find she was short of bologna.

She would give me a dollar, and send me diagonally southeast over the hill (of Carlin Park – location of the town water tower[12] past the swimming pool)) to Garvey's store to get some more bologna. Mrs. Garvey would pull a huge round tube of bologna out of the cooler, heft it over to the butcher table, and cut off a chunk approximating the amount we needed. She would use a huge knife, begin a downward cut, and then seem to be somehow distracted, and erratically conclude the cut haphazardly. She would wrap the chunk (that I thought looked like a trapezoidal cube of roadkill) in waxy white paper, tape it shut, and hand it to me after I paid her.

Once I got the bologna package home, Mom would open it and chuckle at its grotesque shape. Without her asking, I denied any disruption or interference with Mrs. Garvey's work which may have caused the awkward mutilation. It was peculiar to say the least, but we had been spoiled by Harry Siedschlag's store, four blocks farther down Polk Street on Floyd Avenue, that would have produced a neat, tidy, and symmetrical chunk of bologna using Harry's shiny, stainless steel slicing machine. Nevertheless, Mrs. Garvey was closer, her misshapen bologna ground up easily, and it made a tasty sandwich just the same.

Our two barbers offered a very distinctive choice. Depending on whom you selected, what you received was as different as night and day. Shorty Girard gave what my Dad called a "bowl cut," and Jim

---

[11] The recipe for bologna spread included ground up bologna, mayonnaise, and ground pickle or relish. It then and now was and is one of my favorite sandwiches.
[12] The Leeds water tower was felled in 1948, with a deafening boom that left a depression in the hill a couple of feet deep and about the size of half of a football field.

Primm was a master at the lopsided flat top. So you either looked like a doofus or you had to walk leaning to one side or the other depending on the slope of your crew cut. Jim was my preferred choice – he was very personable and seemed to be able to relate to teenagers better than most. One clever innovation in his shop was a bicycle seat that he had rigged up on a frame to fasten to the barber chair – giving him the ability to sit and rotate around the chair while cutting away.

Jim Primm created endless speculations for teenage boys with his colorful tales. He once told some friends and me that sex had a "shelf life." He pointed out that if you put a penny in a jar <u>during</u> your honeymoon every time you made love, and then pulled a penny out <u>following</u> the honeymoon for the same reason, you would never empty the jar. Despite his earthiness and to his credit, Jim was always interested in what we were doing in school and it was fun to gather in his shop to read his magazines and chat with friends.

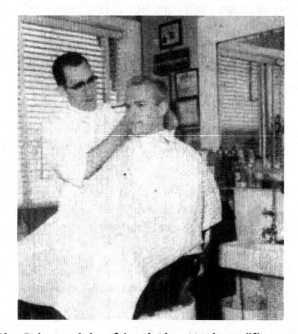

Jim Primm giving friend Alan Hatler a "flat top"

Later, after I acquired my first car, I would drive up to 22nd and Court Street in Sioux City to get my haircuts from Jim Erickson. He wore a flat top (as did most of us) and I thought he knew best how to keep mine from going askew. Nothing worse than a flat-top haircut with a tilt off to port or starboard – it could actually create a serious loss of self-assurance to be walking around with a crummy haircut – or at least I sometimes thought so.

My favorite store was Harry Siedschlag's general store, which was endlessly interesting to a small town kid. Harry sold groceries, produce, meat, clothes, shoes, hardware, candy, appliances, and just about anything else you would want, including peanuts (in the shell) from a large wooden barrel. Mom and Dad always took the three of us (brother Mick, sister Lynda, and me) to Harry's store a few weeks before school started in the fall to get us a new pair of shoes. Harry was a highly successful and persuasive salesman. If the shoes were a mite snug, he'd say, "You'll stretch them out." If they were a mite too big, he'd say, "You'll grow into them." We always bought the shoes. I don't think my feet knew the difference after running around barefoot all summer.

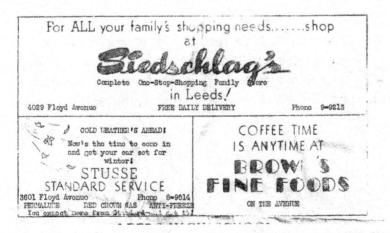

Leeds Merchants' Advertisements in 1955 Football Program

Naturally, Leeds had a tavern, not surprisingly named the "Leeds Tavern," with a giant Hamm's Beer mural on the west side of the building showing the Hamm's[13] bear skating on an ice-blue northern lake surrounded by tall pines. I was excited once to be able to see the sign painter creating this outdoor art masterpiece in our little town. Once, I even had the pleasure of briefly visiting the inside of the tavern when Mom sent me in to get my Dad, where he frequently went after work for a beer or two along with most of the working guys in town. I remember that a draft beer was 10 cents. I must have been young, because I thought that was a lot of money. After my Dad chastised my Mom for sending me into the tavern, I didn't get in there again.

We had fun with the stores occasionally – once we called Mrs. Garvey at her little neighborhood grocery store at the southeast corner of 45th Street and Polk Avenue (phone numbers in those days were only five digits)[14] and asked her the common joke in those days, "Do you have Prince Albert in the can?" (for you younger folks, it was pipe or "roll your own" tobacco that came in a tin). When she said yes, we'd say, "Well, let him out!" We giggled on the floor for a long time on that one. Looking back, I think sometimes we may have been hard up for entertainment.

The Leeds Library was a great resource for young kids like me. Located on Floyd Avenue just east of Central Avenue, it was one of the libraries built with money donated by Scottish-American businessman and philanthropist Andrew Carnegie. Carnegie managed to monopolize

---

[13] Hamm's Beer was advertised as the beer "from the land of sky blue waters."

[14] Phone numbers had an interesting evolution in the number of digits during my youth. In 1946, our phone number was "9727" and in 1950, it added another digit prefix and became "9-9727." Then about 1959, it grew to 7 digits — "239-9727," and in 1965, it evolved into 10 digits, becoming "(712) 239-9727. I have no clue as to who might have that number some 50 years later. If you give it a call, tell them that their phone number has been memorialized in print.

steel production in the United States, and sold his steel enterprises to J. P. Morgan for $480 million, which was about $200 billion in 2012 funds. With his fortune, Carnegie provided grants for 1,689 libraries that were built between 1883 and 1929 in the United States, including a $6500 grant for the Leeds Library. Thanks to Carnegie, many generations in Leeds benefitted greatly from a very fine library within walking distance of nearly everyone in town.

The Leeds Carnegie Library

Leeds was annexed by Sioux City in the late years of the nineteenth century. The Albertson's factory (which manufactured Sioux tools) and Trinity College were located between Leeds and Sioux City, which encouraged the annexation. In recent years, Leeds has become part of the spread of Sioux City dramatically changing its character. However, in 2010 it did my heart good to see that the Des Moines Register's Annual Great Bicycle Ride across Iowa showed Leeds on its map as one of the "towns" that bikers would travel through on their itinerary. Sioux City was mentioned as the stop immediately before Leeds. At last, I finally had some meager documentation to support my claim that I really did grow up in a small town with its own identity putting a stop to my wife's skepticism because her home town population was less than 200 people. [15]

Aerial view of Leeds in 2014

In the aerial view above, it is possible to locate three landmarks in Leeds: (1) my home at 4548 Central Avenue, (2) the commercial section we called "Leeds," and (3) the original site of Leeds High School. In the upper left hand corner the old swimming farm pond can be seen. Just looking at this recent picture, my nostalgia begins to bring up memories of the tree lined streets, turn of the century homes, and the friendliness of neighbors.

The Leeds environment, or experience if you will, enriched all of us who lived there. We had so many "famous" attractions – most of

---

[15] I once bragged to my wife that my high school graduating class consisted of 13 individuals, but she topped that with her class of only 9 graduates.

which we took for granted. Surrounded by farms, Leeds had the internationally famous Jolly Time Popcorn plant in the northeast part of town, the Great Lakes Pipeline tank farm on the east, between U.S. Highway 75[16] and the railroad tracks, the Wincharger Corporation across the street, which was a plant that made wind-powered electric generators many decades before their popularity. After the Wincharger plant closed, my brother Mick and some buddies shot out over a hundred windows in the factory with their BB guns, which caused no small amount of unhappiness for my folks and a licking for Mick.

A few miles south from Leeds down Highway 75 was the Metz Baking Company, where Old Home Bread was baked all day and night, casting the pleasing aroma of baking bread in the area. That was my favorite environmental odor, and it was constantly at war with another familiar fragrance – the Sioux City Stockyards – which was a few more miles down the highway. My Dad always joked that "that was the smell of money." I thought that meant that it was somehow connected to the "root of all evil" or so it seemed.

---

[16] U.S. Highway 75 was called the Blue Star Highway to honor the men and women who served in World War II, including my Dad who served in the Pacific theater in the United States Marine Corps.

II.

Activities: Fun, thrift, and goings-on

"The more that you learn the more places you'll go."
— Dr. Seuss, I *Can Read With My Eyes Shut!*

Living in Leeds was a rich mix of memorable activities and events. We lived a simple life – not impoverished, but devoid of all tangible manifestations of wealth – in a very basic home in a very basic neighborhood. Dad was a truck driver until 1948, when he lost an eye in a horrible accident involving a meat hook in a semi-trailer while transporting sides of beef from the Sioux City Stockyards to the Black Hills of South Dakota. The sides of beef he hauled were around 150 pounds or more, and they hung on meat hooks. Dad, who was immensely strong, would sling the sides of beef onto his shoulder, and lift them to unhook them, and carry them into the store's meat department. While whirling around with one of the sides, he tangled with one of the hooks – losing his left eye and nearly his life as well as his commercial Driver's License.

With that tragedy in 1948 (and no worker's compensation in those days), Dad then joined with his Dad (my Granddad) in the building trades, and became a carpenter. Always very handy, he could do it all – woodworking, concrete work, wiring, plumbing, etc. He and Gramps made a great team, with Gramps providing the craftsman skills of finish carpentry. I remember being very impressed when I heard that Dad earned $3.25 an hour as a union carpenter. That seemed like a ton of money to me at the time. In actuality, that was about $550 a month (about $1200 a month or $14,000 per year in 2014 dollars) – if he worked steadily, which he seldom did. Work in the Sioux City area for carpenters was largely seasonal, with little demand in the winter months.

There were lean times. Mom's creativity and thriftiness provided us with inexpensive meals — meatloaf, macaroni and cheese, and goulash — which were rib-sticking good, and economical at the same time. Fridays, since Mom was Catholic, were always meat-free meaning fish, tuna casserole, mac and cheese, potato soup or something similar. My brother Mick and I knew that when we had potato soup, it meant an early bedtime since we'd be hungry again after a few hours and the only way to stave that off was to just go to sleep. However, one thing we had plenty of and we enjoyed immensely was an unending supply of peanut butter and bread.[17] We could always make ourselves a snack with those two ingredients, which was OK to Mom, since she believed in an open kitchen.

In the down times during the winter months, Dad had a clever plan. He set up a shop in the garage and made a boat by hand. The next spring and summer, we'd use the boat for water skiing, fishing, and the like, but he'd sell it in the fall to get money for the dearth of income in the cold months. One boat I remember had over 3000 brass screws that he drove by hand with an old Yankee ratcheting screwdriver! [18]

Mom was a stay-at-home mother as most mothers were in those days. I can never remember any time when I came home from school that Mom wasn't there. Having her greet me after school was very comforting, and she always wanted to know what I was learning in school. That was real bonding. One interesting characteristic of Mom her en-

---

[17] Bread was usually Old Home Bread, Wonder Bread, or bread from the Omar Bread man, who drove door to door in a van delivering bread, pies etc. that were baked in Omaha, 100 miles south. Other delivery companies included Roberts Dairy, Jewel Tea Company, Watkins kitchen things, and the Fuller Brush Company. Door to door deliveries in recent times have almost become a thing of the past.

[18] The Iowa climate, both weather wise and economic, finally prompted Dad to leave Iowa for construction work in California in January of 1961 at the age of 44. He never missed another season of work and worked every day he wanted to work until he turned 80 years of age and finally decided to retire.

tire life was her love of games – especially word games – Scrabble, Boggle, and Hangman. She also loved crossword puzzles and using vocabulary that stretched my own.

Mom's activities outside the home were limited, due in large part to the responsibilities of managing the home and family. She was active in the Parent Teachers' Association, and volunteered for many school programs and projects. She even joined the Leeds Variety Bowling Team, which was one evening a week after dinner at the Sioux Village Bowl. The team was made up of her friends, and my memory is that Mom enjoyed the camaraderie.

Mom's Bowling Team 1955

Top row: Ruth Gardner, Imogene Palmerton,
Wilma Poston (Mom), Frances Babcock;
Bottom row: Lila Harward, Lola Brown, Norma Townsend

Once all three of us kids were at the high school (remember it was a grade 7-12 school), Mom did take a part time job at the S&H stamp store. I'm sure kids of today won't know what S&H stamps were, but in the post war days, they were akin to earning rewards for purchasing with a credit card or shopping a certain store. The retail stores in town would buy little green stamps from Sperry & Hutchinson and give them as bonuses with every purchase based on the amount you bought. The more you bought the more stamps you got. People would save the stamps in a special book until they had enough stamp books to go to an S&H store and redeem the books for merchandise. Eventually you saved up enough stamps, licked and pasted them into the Saver's Book, and toddled down to the redemption center with a sore tongue and trade them in for merchandise.

S&H Green Stamps and the Saver's Book

Mom's job was to greet the customer, collect their stamps, verify the quantity, and exchange the stamps for all kinds of things – kitchen utensils, tools, games, recreational equipment, bikes, etc. The S&H stamp program was very popular in the 20th Century. It was a good job for Mom, because she could schedule her work hours around our school schedules and pick up a few dollars in the process. It was also fun to visit her at the S&H store in downtown Sioux City, where we could feast our eyes on all kinds of tantalizing things. It was entertainment at its best.

In the days before high school, our main source of entertainment was exploring the outdoors, which we did extensively. We did have radio, and it was special to listen to dramas on radio – making us use our imagination greatly. I remember shows like *The Lone Ranger, The Green Hornet, The Shadow, Mr. and Mrs. North* mysteries, and many others. *The Arthur Godfrey Show* woke us up and sent us off to school each morning. Games we played were made up by us as we went along – we had no trouble making our own entertainment. Today's kids spend huge amounts of time viewing screens by themselves, something we couldn't imagine in our youth. We had a humongous "social network" all over Leeds without any digital equipment. Imagine that!

Other conditions of life in those days were dramatically different for us than what they are today. Here are just a few things of note:

- We had glass milk bottles, which we washed and returned for the dairy to clean for the next delivery (which came to our door). Note that this was "recycling" before it was so called.
- We walked or rode our bike to school, the grocery store, church, and mostly wherever we had to go in town.
- Baby diapers were cloth, and they were washed after every use and dried on a clothesline outside.
- We didn't have TV until I was about 14 years old, but we had a radio with great serial programs which came on weekly.
- We mowed the grass with a push mower – human power instead of gas power.
- We refilled our writing pens with ink instead of throwing away a ball point pen after use.
- We "made" our own margarine, by buying white oleo in a plastic bag, and then breaking open a capsule of yellow food coloring inside the bag and squeezing it repeatedly to color the margarine until it looked like butter.
- Our dining room had a single light bulb hanging from the ceiling to light our dinners.

And then people might say, "We didn't conserve in those days?" Ironically, we did – more than anyone does today.

Life in Leeds was characterized partly by the history and geography of the town itself, but also partly by our close interface with the farms and agricultural lands surrounding our little community. Exploring the countryside was the source of unending pleasure for me as a boy. We ran up and down the hills, explored the creeks, and tramped through the wooded areas. The profusion of wildlife was amazing to behold. We encountered opossums, badgers, skunks, rabbits, gophers, pheasants, garter snakes, bull snakes, moles, pigeons, doves, bullhead catfish and carp in the streams, geese and ducks, and many more.

My dog Lucky, some hybrid combination[19] of Spitz and Collie, was white with a patch of black on his rump. He had a tan patch over his right eye, which extended over his left ear, and a tail that curved up over his back. He was my faithful companion everywhere I went. He wanted to accompany me so badly that he would run in front of my bike barking like mad. He was so close that I actually drove over him a couple of times with my bike – no harm to him, but I always took a spill. Siedschlag's General Store held a dog beauty contest once in Leeds Park (41st and Central) and I enrolled Lucky. He took first place – for the longest tail — and Bill Siedschlag awarded him a blue ribbon to prove it. It was a proud moment for Lucky and for me.

Lucky was a very durable animal. He loved to run alongside me on my bicycle, and occasionally he would cut in front of me. A couple of times, I actually collided with him, causing a big spill. On the dirt road, I would get dirty and somewhat bruised, but Lucky simply got up and kept going. One time, I ran over him – bumpity bump – and took an-

---

[19] Dogs of unknown mixed breeds were often referred to as "Heinz 57," denoting a complex mixture of heredity.

other spill, but again Lucky bounded up and kept going without a whimper. He was with someone he loved, and he was willing to take a few lumps to keep the relationship alive and well. What a dog.

My Faithful Friend, Lucky, by My Side (c/ 1950)[20]

Lucky was really my first dog. He was eminently less stupid than many people I've met, and as Eugene O'Neill once said, "Dogs do not ruin their sleep worrying about how to keep the objects they have, or to obtain the

---

[20] First, check out those jeans – they were long, in the improbable chance that I grew 6-8 inches before they wore out. Also, note the mailbox beside the front door. In those days, the mail carrier (we used to say 'mailman') would climb our hill, struggle up over 20 stairs with a heavy bag full of mail, and deliver the mail right to the front door. Mail delivery is much different today.

objects they have not. There is nothing of value they have to bequeath except their love and their faith." Ever since, the only times I have been without a dog, were when in college or serving in the military.

I've learned about marsupial mammals by watching a 'possum carry her young in her pouch, learned about avoiding skunks when I got sprayed full force pulling a spotted skunk[21] out of a hole in the ground tail first with its weaponry aimed at me, then I learned about the ferocity of badgers when I cornered one but his fangs and growls kept me at bay while he dug a hole in a clay bank in which to hide, I learned about hunting by accompanying my Dad hunting for pheasants and rabbits,[22] I learned to fish in the muddy rivers and creeks for bullhead

---

[21] My incident with a spotted skunk (sometimes erroneously called a civet cat), which is now nearly extirpated in Iowa, was an experience that I vividly remember six decades later. It took place while visiting my Clark cousins (their Mom, Dorothy, was Dad's younger sister) — Gary, Gail, Randy, and Melvin (Kip came later) — in their Sioux Falls, South Dakota, home on the old WWII Army Air Force base (now the Sioux Falls Commercial Airport). Gary – five months my junior — said he had a trap line out for rabbits and raccoons. I agreed to accompany him to check the traps to see if he had any success. It was winter, about 10° below zero, with a fresh wind, not unusual for South Dakota, and we bundled up and trudged out into the arctic-like conditions. We came to a chain attached to a trap, but the trap was down in a large hole out of sight. Expecting to get a rabbit, we started pulling on the chain, when the back end of a spotted skunk came into view and immediately sprayed both Gary and me. The wind was in our faces, so we didn't smell a thing. Gary dispatched the animal, and we trudged back to his home, proud of his triumph (pelts were worth a few dollars then). We got to the door of the Clark home, which was a converted Army barracks, and opened the door and started in. My mother immediately jumped up and started screaming, "Get out! Go back outside!" We complied, and she then told us to take off our clothes (except for our underwear) and bury them in a snow drift out front. That was a real challenge. We hopped on the cold tundra back into the house, only to go immediately into a bath, head to toe, with Lava Soap. I never did find out how much money Gary got for that pelt, but whatever it was, it wasn't worth it.

[22] One of my Dad's rules about hunting was that we never shot anything that we didn't plan to eat. That was an interesting lesson when I killed a couple of dozen pigeons, with my Red Ryder BB gun, in Mr. Philpott's barn haymow (up at the end of Central Avenue north of our house and 46th Street about 200 yards) at his request. He didn't want pigeon droppings on his hay (food for his cattle). Dad's rule was that since I had killed them, I had to eat them. Mom helped me clean them, and she baked up a pan of "squabs" (pigeons) consisting of the breast meat which was the size of a couple of tablespoons each. Fortunately, Dad and everyone else joined in the repast, but I never shot another pigeon. Once was enough.

catfish with my Dad, my Grandad, and my Grandma Poston (who loved to fish), and I learned the economic value of trapping gophers and turning in the front paws to the County Game and Fish Department which paid us a 2-cent bounty per pair. What could be learned in Leeds and its environs was endless and meaningful.

When we fished – usually along the Floyd River located just outside the east side of Leeds or over in the Sioux River just above the confluence with the Mighty Missouri River or along the Missouri River's former channel (an ox-bow lake) south of town called Brown's Lake – our catch was almost universally the Bullhead Catfish. They were usually a pound in weight or so, and ornery as all get out. Their dorsal fin had a nasty and sharp "thorn" in it which could do some damage to unprotected hands. They were tasty though. Our meatless Catholic meals on Friday often highlighted bullheads. They were a very economical meal and went well with pan-fried potatoes. If we caught a carp, we just tossed it back. Once in a great while, we'd catch a small bass and I remember even catching a walleye pike, which was really special.

Bill and Mick in Dad's First Boat, the "Lynda Kay" c.1949.

Fishing on Brown's Lake was always fun. Dad would let us use the boat sans his 5hp Evinrude motor to navigate by sweat and exertion. The lake was a distasteful "root beer" color, but exploration was exciting for young boys.

Don Johnson[23] and I, while visiting his grandparents in Elk Point, South Dakota, bought a "gigging" fork at the hardware store for a dime or so, fastened it on a broom handle, and used it to "gig" fish in the slough that was southwest of town. I remember those days every time I'm driving on Interstate 29, which goes right over where the slough was located. Despite the adventure and fun in catching them, any carp went back in the water since they were not good to eat – too many bones.

West of our home, out in what was called Fairacres, we discovered the perfect pond to go skinny dipping. A bunch of us (all boys) would hike on the dusty dirt road (46th Street) about 1 miles west to what is now named Rustin Street and down the hill to the southwest and there it was.

We swam in that pond many times, and there was nothing more re-freshing on a hot, humid summer day that a dip in the cool pond. We just had to be careful to avoid the "cow pies."

We also would occasionally go east on 46th Street, which was a dirt road the opposite direction, about a mile and a half down to the Floyd River and skinny dip there too.

---

[23] Don Johnson and his brother, Larry, were always good friends and fun to be around. Don and I conducted many an exploratory excursion into the woods, rivers, hills, and valleys around Leeds. Their mother, Norma, was a wonderful hostess for our gatherings in their basement. Unfortunately, Don was seriously injured in midlife and confined to a wheelchair before he passed on in 2008 at age 70.

Our Fairacres Swimming Hole

The special treat about swimming in the Floyd River was that there were lots of sandbars when the river was low. The shoreline was heavily wooded in those days (before the river was channelized after the 1953 flood) and the trees were laced with long vines that we would use to swing out over the river and drop into the water. It was great fun, and it made us feel like Tarzan. Ironically, the river was heavily silted and occasionally still had some sewage and disgusting debris from towns upstream so it's a wonder that we didn't all get typhoid fever.

There were other dangers in skinny dipping too. Snapping turtles lived in the murky waters, and testimony to that danger was once when my Dad and Grandad experienced the effects of a snapping turtle's powerful jaws. While they were fishing in the Sioux River – the tributary of the Mighty Missouri River on the west side of Sioux City – they caught some bullhead catfish, and had

The Intrepid Skinny-Dippers

them on a stringer hanging down into the water at the side of their boat. Soon, there was a commotion, and they pulled the stringer out of the water to discover that some hefty bites had been taken out of one of the bullheads leaving only the fish's head – thanks to a snapping turtle. I always feared that a snapper might take my manhood. The thought gives me chills even today.

The Iowa Alligator Snapping Turtle

After hearing Dad tell about the fish's fate, I was always a mite leery when swimming sans clothes in dark murky rivers – which would accurately describe waters of the Floyd River.[24] Some things just don't require risking.

Speaking of skinny dipping, once in a while, usually on a Saturday in the winter months, we would hop the Sioux City bus to downtown Sioux City[25] and go to the YMCA to skinny dip in the indoor pool. Believe me when I say that we skinny dipped there too! We were all young boys of course, and we were told that it was more sanitary to go nude in the indoor pool than it was

Boys swimming nude at the YMCA, 1951

---

[24] The Floyd River was located on the east side of Leeds and it flowed south to the Mighty Missouri River near the Sioux City Stockyards. Its waters were always murky with eroded farm land soil from upstream. Growing up between these two rivers, I swam, fished, boated, and ice skated on one or the other frequently. A richer set of experiences for youth could not have ever been found.

[25] The Sioux City Bus Company came out to Leeds, and made a loop through town, stopping at 44th Street and Central Avenue to pick up passengers. Fare was 5¢ for a one way ride down to 4th and Pierce Streets.

wearing clothing. The official policy was to swim *au naturel.* Nobody paid any attention to it, and it seemed very natural to swim without soggy swim suits. We just frolicked in the water until we had to get dressed, hop the bus and get back out to Leeds.

In the wintertime, we were especially blessed with an outdoor ice skating area on the south side of Floyd Avenue, kitty corner from Grover Wilkins drug store in the area between the Dairy Queen and Keith Wixon's Conoco gas station. The field was flooded, it froze quickly, and an "ice house" was placed on the north east end with benches on all four walls and a pot-bellied stove in the middle. It was a great place to put on your skates or warm up in between skating sessions. I have many nice memories about skating like crazy in below-zero weather and then hurrying into the ice house to warm up. Those pot-bellied stoves used to get so hot, they glowed in the dark.

Keith Wixon's Conoco Station
(NE of the Ice Rink on Tyler St. and Floyd Ave.)

Once in a great while in the winter, I would join some of my cousins from Crescent Park on Sioux City's west side at the bottom of Prospect Hill, where we would walk across Gordon Drive and skate on small estuaries and inlets of the Missouri River. For some reason, there always was ample thickness of the ice and I remember no mishaps ever occurring. It was fun to skate from one frozen sandbar to another. Even more fun when we made a bonfire.

On the east side of the Leeds skating rink was a railroad track, which served the Great Northern, Milwaukee Road, Illinois Central, and Chicago Northwestern Lines between Sioux City and Minneapolis/St. Paul. The trains were always something to watch, as the steam engines chugged through Leeds, spewing heavy black smoke as they moved north toward LeMars.

Great Northern Locomotive Moving Fast c. 1949

The proximity of the tracks provided some fascinating, if dangerous, entertainment for the boys of Leeds. For example, you could "hop" the train in Sioux City and ride it back out about five miles to Leeds and then jump off. That is, if the train wasn't going too fast to jump. A boy named Syl(vester) Gagnon reportedly had that very experience, though the story may be apocryphal. The legend goes that when the train got to Leeds it had already picked up a good head of steam and

Syl was trapped on the train and allegedly had to ride it north to LeMars before it slowed down enough for him to jump off. If he did that, and I don't doubt it, I have no idea how he got home – 25 miles back south.

I know that we occasionally hopped one of the trains, slowing down as it was headed toward Sioux City, shortly before dark and hopped off at the spot near the Highway 75 Drive-In Theater. By then, the train had slowed down enough that we could dismount without too much trouble. Although, I heard that Larry Bohlke had slipped and the toe of his shoe got squashed by the train wheel.

Chicago &
North Western Caboose

Of course, in a small town, if people didn't know the facts, it wasn't un-common to make something up. So I can't swear that happened. Never-theless, after the movie, we were on our own to hitch-hike up Highway 75 (the Blue Star Highway) to the Leeds viaduct or the Great Lakes Pipeline tank farm and walk home from there.

One hot summer day Tom Hooker and I walked those tracks south to-ward Sioux City where they crossed the Floyd River just above Spring-dale, got off at the bridge, and skinny dipped in the Floyd off a beautiful sand bar that had been created after the heavy spring flows. Warm sun, warm water, hot clean sand — it was one of the best sites for skinny dipping we had ever found in Leeds.

Winter seldom impeded our quest for adventure. Once cold February day, when the schools were closed because of the weather, a bunch of us hitchhiked about 80 miles north up Highway 75 to Luverne, Minnesota just for the heck of it.[26] We had enough money to send a 2¢ postcard home to prove we had been there, but the temperature had dropped to 10° below zero, and the rides back weren't readily available. We once waited on the highway near Rock Rapids for what seemed an eternity before some Good Samaritan took pity on us and picked us up. We finally arrived back home after supper time. It was an adventure that I never wanted to repeat.[27] Sometimes I reflect on such shenanigans, and wonder how any of us made it past puberty.

---

[26] Late in life, I read about the immaturity of the teenager's frontal lobe, which causes various levels of impaired judgment. I'm sure we were victims of that affliction, considering some of the stunts we executed.

[27] Not surprisingly, Leeds was the mechanism for many lessons learned while growing up – some painful, some embarrassing, and some exhilarating. Many of these random thoughts are organized to hopefully entertain my grandchildren and find them witty if not informative. Of course, those reckless and foolhardy experiences are not worthy of emulation in the high-speed world of today.

III.

Between the Rivers: Excitement, enjoyment, and enthusiasm

"Youth comes but once in a lifetime."
- <u>Henry Wadsworth Longfellow</u>

Leeds is located in the northwest quadrant of Iowa, framed a few miles south by the great "Big Muddy" as Meriwether Lewis and William Clark called the Missouri River as they came through headed north-west in August of 1804. On the east side of Leeds was the Floyd River, named for US Army Sergeant Charles Floyd, who was the only member of the Lewis and Clark expedition to die on the momentous exploration of the headwaters of the Missouri and Columbia Rivers. He died, of what was thought later to be appendicitis, right at the confluence of the

Sgt. Charles Floyd Monument

(now named) Floyd and Missouri rivers, where he was buried (marked by a huge obelisk monument erected in 1910 overlooking the conflu-ence of the Floyd River with the Missouri River). A few miles west of Leeds, actually on the western boundary of Iowa, was the Sioux River, a sizable tributary of the "Might Mo."

Of course, the Lewis and Clark expedition of the lands acquired in the Louisiana Purchase of 1803 preceded creation of the Iowa Territory in 1838. The Iowa Territory originally was all of the land between the Mississippi and Missouri Rivers from the northern edge of the Missouri Territory all the way north to the Canadian border. However, state-hood for Iowa, which was approved by the U.S. Congress on December 28, 1846, meant a constraint to its current configuration and boundaries. I remember the year of statehood very clearly, not from personal experience obviously, but due to my participation in the Iowa Centennial celebration in the summer of 1946. As a member of the Sioux City Sons of the American Legion Drum and Bugle Corps, I participated in celebration at Morningside College's football stadium, where I remember exciting reenactments of Iowa history. I especially remember a race between "settlers" driving covered wagons with a team of horses, re-enacting the rush to homestead the free land in Iowa.[28]

Most references to Iowa include it in the "flatlands" of the United States, but for those of us who were born and nurtured here, it is anything but. For those who don't know, Iowa derives its name from the Ioway people, one of the many Native American tribes that occupied the state at the time of European exploration, and its meaning is often referred to as the "land between the rivers." Its geography is a fascinating combination of prairie, forests, glacier moraines, rivers, gulches, ravines, hills, valleys, some 54 rivers, and innumerable ponds and lakes.[29]

Leeds' geography provided lots of educational benefits without much pretension. For example, most of the north-south streets in Leeds were named after 19th Century U.S. presidents, including Jefferson, Monroe, Madison, Van Buren, Harrison, Tyler, Polk, Grant, Garfield, Arthur, and Cleveland. Riding my bike across Leeds east or west always gave me a reminder that we were part of something bigger than our small town as we learned a smidgen of American history. And ride our bikes we did. I don't think there's a corner of Leeds and much of Woodbury County that we didn't explore on our bikes. I can remem-

---

[28] Homesteading was a means of obtaining free public land by living on and improving their claim of 160 acres for five years.

[29] For trivia buffs, Iowa is the only state that has a state abbreviation that consists of two vowels (IA).

ber peddling all the way across the loess hills west of Leeds about 7 or 8 miles to visit my widowed Irish grandmother in Crescent Park, a section of Sioux City on the northwest side at the corner of 28th and George Streets located in the watershed of Prairie Creek.

The residents of Leeds were a diverse mixture of not only ethnic groups but also economic strata. There were mostly northern European families, including Irish, Polish, English, German, Norwegian, Italian, and Swedish families as I recall, as well as an occasional family of Iberian extraction and a few others. In those days, the population contained few, if any, minority groups, although I always wondered about where "Shorty" Domisic's (pronounced "Dom-ah-see") heritage lay.

My own heritage was a mystery to me at that time but I knew my Mom's Irish and German forebears had come to this country in the latter part of the 19th century. I didn't learn until I was much older that my Dad's English forebears had come to this country in the very early 18th century (circa 1703) and that I had two direct ancestors – William Patton and Solomon Poston – who served in Washington's army during the Revolutionary War.

That piece of knowledge was unknown by my Dad until late in life, but he did know that his Great Grandmother Elizabeth Kincaid Poston (later Clymer) had come to Iowa from Virginia in 1865 (after losing both the "War Between the States" and at the same time losing her husband — my Great-Great Grandfather — Fielden Lane Poston). How I wish I had known about that family history when my friend John Dreves would boast about his ancestors in the Revolutionary War. Isn't it strange that some things about our histories are frequently unknown within the family but actually were potential points of pride in our heritage? If only we had known.[30]

Leeds had a seasonal Dairy Queen that provided a cold rich dessert in the hot summer months. It was owned and operated by Mr. and Mrs. Elmer Kingsbury who lived in the back of the store, and they went to Florida in the winter. They were an interesting couple, and very pleasant. Since Mrs. Kingsbury was about a head taller and 100 pounds heavier than her husband, Elmer, we were inclined to refer to him as "Elmer Fudd" – the short chubby character in Bugs Bunny cartoons – with affection of course. The Kingsburys hired many girls in Leeds to work at the Dairy Queen, and the girls wore translucent white dresses, which conjured up interesting mental images for teenage boys.

The Dairy Queen cones were only a nickel; a dollar went a lot farther in those days. We could satiate our sweet tooth for little cash. Down in Sioux City on Saturday mornings, it was possible to get a huge box of cookies from the Johnson Biscuit Company that contained factory rejects for a buck (dollar). The box was about 15" wide, tall, and long. There was no choice of type of cookie, and they weren't always pretty, but the taste wasn't spoiled at all.

Behind the Dairy Queen was a railroad depot with a telegraph operator that manned the post. The Illinois Central Depot, on the north side of the railroad tracks, was south of the intersection of 41st Street and

---

[30] I will never forget John Dreves, a member of my 5th Grade class, who hadn't come to my 10th birthday party, ostensibly because he didn't have a gift to bring. Mom called his mom and asked her to send John over – no gift required. He came, but he did have a gift — a small package of home-made peanut brittle, with a quarter in it! Wow. 25 cents! That was the most money I ever had held in my hand, and I thought I was rich! Thank you John! I found out that quarter would be worth about $3.50 today, not including any numismatic collector value. Amazing how such a small amount could have brought such delight – most probably, it was due to our lack of disposable income in those days and the power of a small amount of money. A Snicker bar was only 5¢, a Dairy Queen cone cost 5¢ (see above), and 1¢ would buy a bubble gum or a jaw breaker. If you don't know what a jaw breaker is, ask your grandfather.

Floyd Avenue. There were a lot of trains that went through Leeds, and the station was clearly marked with the name of our town. In the early days, an Illinois Central train traveled back and forth between Leeds and Sioux City – a distance of less than five miles. It was popular as a depot for many years, but after the First World War, it became a communication and switching station, with a telegraph operator ensconced within. Trains never stopped in Leeds after that; they slowed down, but they never stopped.

Leeds Depot: Illinois Central Railroad 1950

The agent in the Depot was Ben Kinard, and one memorable visit involved Ben showing us how his telegraph system worked. His grasp of dots and dashes was enthralling to boys like me who were interested in the "latest" technology. Other forms of transportation came to Leeds, including the electric street car, which stopped on the corner of Tyler and Floyd Avenue, by Grover Wilkins' drug store, up until the late 1940's.

Sioux City Streetcar stops at Floyd Avenue and Tyler Streets c. 1947

Riding the streetcar down to Sioux City was a rare treat. The ride was 5 cents, and it went back and forth several times a day. It wasn't too adept at turns, but it moved briskly. I wasn't old enough to ride it unaccompanied, but I rode it with Aunt Karen once or twice, my cousin Colleen a time or two as well, but Mom accompanied me most of the time. In the wintertime, the streetcar was heated with a pot-bellied coal stove in the middle of the car like the one that heated our house, which made me feel right at home.[31]

In the picture above, you can see Grover Wilkins' drug store on the left, and just in front of the store on the curb (bottom left of the picture), you can see the water fountain[32] that flowed continually. Note

---

[31] The streetcar system survived until about 1948, when it was displaced by the Sioux City Transit Bus System. The fare was the same.

[32] The water fountain was cleverly designed – it had a bubbler in a bowl that ran continually on a pipe stand about three feet high. Water than dropped into the surrounding bowl was

also the Burke Lumber Yard in the back of the picture where Bob Harward and I once unloaded coal from a train car – one block at a time.

Some summers, a carnival would come to Leeds and set up on Floyd Avenue in the skating rink area. The usual rides were there – Ferris wheel, tilt-a-whirl, etc. They also had a number of challenge games, like throwing darts at a wall pinned with many balloons for prizes given the number of balloons you broke, or swinging a billiard ball hung on a chain away from a bowling pin to see if you could knock the pin over when the ball swung back. Mick was about 15 years old at the time, and had been working in a summer job, saving $12, which he lost at the bowling ball booth in something less than 5 minutes. Something in the ball made it swerve away from the pin in its return trajectory. Each time, he lost a dollar. He was encouraged to try again, and since it seemed so simple, Mick gave it another go. Twelve tries later, Mick was devastated and he cried. We both learned a bitter lesson that day about gambling. This game was definitely our first experience with a scam.

At another carnival, in South Sioux City, an enticing attraction had an impact for Bob Harward and me. With our blighted frontal cranial lobes, we fell victim to our urges, and both got tattoos for $5 apiece. The tattoos were identical flying eagles with a banner in their talons with our names on them. Mine said "Bill," and Bob's was supposed to be Bob. However, the tattoo artist made a "P" in Bob's tattoo, and started to make another letter. Bob said something, and the artist said, "What did you say your name was?" Of course it was Bob, but the artist said "well, I thought you said Phil!" Bob almost got somebody else's name on his upper arm – permanently.

---

captured in a drain pipe that filled another bowl at ground level for dogs and cats. It was equipped with an overflow that went in the sewer.

The tattoo turned out to be a serious regret, since afterward I got an infection, which required treatment and a doctor's visit. About 15 years later, after continued feelings of embarrassment I had my tattoo removed, and unbeknownst to me, so did Bob at about the same time. We must have had the same crummy feeling about the body art. Lesson learned.

When I was about 11 or so, I wanted a sword for Halloween. I made one out of a rod removed from one of our window shades. Window shades are seldom seen anymore. I carved the wooden rod very carefully, and painted it with aluminum paint. I thought it was great and I imagined that I was a pirate out of a Robert Louis Stevenson novel – at least until I accidentally broke it at Robert Lee's 11th birthday party, held around Halloween in 1949. Robert's mother was very helpful in repairing my sword, providing some white first aid tape to hold it together temporarily. It was a big improvement, but somehow it made me uncomfortable – I think an early symptom of my perfectionism was arising.

Robert was a classmate at Hawthorne School, along with Mary Julia Petty, Janice Janson, Richard Whitlock, John Dreves, and many others that I never saw after our sixth grade class moved to Leeds High School for the seventh grade in January, 1950. I've often thought of so many classmates that have come in and gone out of my life, and what became of them. Attrition was a factor in those days, substantiated by the fact that we entered Leeds High with 22 students in our 7th grade class, we "inherited" a few along the way from earlier classes, but graduated six years later with only 13 survivors – 11 boys and 2 girls. A plethora of circumstances reduced our numbers, including military service (a noble alternative), marriage (not always a noble alternative), employment, relocation, and many other things.

Leeds High School Graduation Class: January 20, 1957

From left to right: Me, Wayne Harrison, Bob Thews, Noel (Red) Painter, Tom Hooker, Donovon Rarick, Bill Owings, Lilas Blumer, Larry Rees, Gloria Spalding, Charles Carmen, Dick Landers, Joe Conley).

It was no secret that unexpected maternity took a few girls out of school from time to time, since pregnancy comprised grounds for expulsion of the girl, but not the boy. Ironically, six decades later in schools, pregnant girls not only may continue with their studies in school but also they can receive pre- and post-natal care for their babies in school facilities. Times do change. Ironically, many of those "shotgun" marriages we witnessed in high school were still intact at our all-school reunion 50 years later – that's a model of love and commitment for any marriage – truly beating the contemporary average.

Media in my childhood was far different than it is in modern-day times. The ball point pen was invented about 1950, which became a quick and easy approach to written communication. Before the ball point, we used liquid ink in small bottles to fill a pen, which usually leaked. The pens were apt to run out of ink frequently as well.

On occasional Saturdays, Dad would give Mick and me a quarter each to go to a movie in downtown Sioux City. This was a huge media event for us. We would walk down to the corner of 44th Street and Central Avenue, by the Lutheran Church, and catch the Sioux City bus to downtown – fare was 5¢. Downtown, we'd go to the aged, almost squalid, Iowa Theater on Jackson Street south of 4th Street. Admission was 10¢, and popcorn was a nickel. We would see a double feature movie, most of the time westerns and rarely in color, plus usually a cartoon (Tom and Jerry, Donald Duck, Mickey Mouse, etc.), and a serial. Serials were movies that had been cut into segments of 15-20 minutes, which would be shown one at a time each week in chronological order. Of course, it was motivation to come back week after week, which we weren't able to do. However, it didn't matter, because each segment provided a quick review of the history of the movie to that point, and it was easy to catch up.

Normally, Mick and I each had 5¢ remaining to get back home by bus. But once in a great while, temptation would lead us astray and we'd spend the remaining nickel on a Snicker bar, Boston Baked Beans, Milk Duds, or something similar. Then we were broke. We had a survival mechanism that usually was successful, though. In those days, parking meters collected nickels on the downtown streets, and some drivers would put an extra nickel in just in case their time expired and the police officer would push the extra nickel in. It was called "plugging." Our scheme was to walk down the streets, slapping the back of each meter and occasionally ejecting a nickel. In ten or fifteen minutes we'd have our bus fare home. Naturally, the consequences to some poor driver who may have gotten a parking ticket never rose to our consciousness. Wrongly, we didn't associate it with wrongdoing until later in life.

Electronic media was limited to radio until about 1950, when television came to Iowa via Omaha. However, Sioux City didn't get its own

TV station until March 9, 1953, when KVTV, channel 9, signed on as western Iowa's first television station. Before that, we were accustomed to getting clear radio stations from far away, especially at night, including a station in Del Rio, Texas, and another closer to home, WNAX radio in Yankton, South Dakota, and the powerful WHO Radio in Des Moines.[33] I was enthralled with radio programs like *The Shadow, The Jack Benny Show, The Green Hornet, Dick Tracy, The Lone Ranger, and Sky King.* Exciting stuff for a kid in the early 1950's.

The first television set I ever saw was about in 1950. Dad told Mick and me to get in the back of his pickup, and we rode down to 4220 Polk Street (about 4 blocks) and picked up Grandpa Poston. We then drove down to 21st Street and crossed Sioux City to the west side and stopped at the home of "Ray-De-O-Ray." Ray-De-O-Ray was the name of an appliance sales and service store that specialized in radios and radio repair. The owner, Ray Kennedy, I believe had obtained the first TV set in Sioux City. We kids stood outside on his porch, looking in through the window into his living room with wonder at this huge box with a small video screen, and watched our first program in black and white. It was some kind of a musical show. The station was from Omaha, 100 miles away, so Ray had this tall antenna in his back yard to capture the signal. It was awe-inspiring, but we had no idea what technology that would unleash years later.

When TV arrived at our house in 1952, I was in the 8th grade, and we could only get black and white grainy pictures from two stations in Omaha, on a TV set that was about 3 feet wide, tall, and deep, with a tiny screen about 12 inches measured diagonally. Dad put our reception tower at the top of our house, nearly three stories above the ground. Some people who could afford it, like Radio Ray, erected tow-

---

[33] WHO Radio in Des Moines, Iowa, earned distinction some years later when its former sportscaster in the 1930's became our 40th President – Ronald Reagan.

ers in their yard up to about 50 feet above ground, so their picture was clearer. We didn't care – we had our own TV.

As I mentioned above, about a year later, TV for much of northwest Iowa, northeast Nebraska, and southeast South Dakota, emanated from Sioux City. Despite the modest economic status of Leeds residents, most homes had TV in their homes by the time I graduated from high school. Despite the very large, heavy wooden boxes and small screens of early television sets, they changed everything then and continue to do so today.

Exploration in our area was ever-present and our "Daniel Boone" inquisitiveness was applied all too frequently. There were so many interesting things to explore – like the storm sewer which started at the top of Harrison Street (one block west on 46th Street from our home). It was about five feet in diameter, and it ran all the way to the Floyd River, about three miles away. Walking into it was like entering a dark, damp, and scary cave. As we progressed deeper into the sewer pipe, faint streaks of light appeared every 100 yards or so from manhole covers and street level drains into the sewer. Most exciting was finding a bat colony that had moved into the sewer and hung from the ceiling and walls of the sewer inlet columns. One of the creepy findings we discovered was that bats have fangs, which they will display even while sleeping when someone flashes a flashlight on them up close. I decided to leave them alone after that.

Prairie rattlesnakes live even today in the Loess Hills part of Iowa, which extend from the Council Bluffs area east of the Missouri River, all the way up to Leeds and beyond. I learned this hitherto unknown fact when my dog, Lucky, was going nuts in the tall bluestem prairie grass east of our house on the edge of Carlin Park. He was hopping around, barking like crazy – sounding like he'd cornered a badger. My investigation ended after I ran through the hip-high blue stem prairie grass to his location, and heard the distinctive rattle of the snake's tail.

I had never heard it before, but it couldn't be anything else. I grabbed Lucky, and we scooted back to safer turf. That hill of prairie grass burned later that summer, after some bone-headed motorist tossed a lighted cigarette out of a car headed east on 46th Street. After the fire occurred, I screwed up enough courage to explore the charred hill, but never found the snake. Because of that snake though, there were no gopher holes, mole tunnels, or field mice in that area either.

What strikes me now about some of our experiences is that we were largely unsupervised, we roamed unhindered, and we were unencumbered in activities – very unlike present-day children. We definitely live in a different time zone today.

A few of our explorations were quasi-scientific. One of my close friends, who shall remain nameless (I swore to take the secret of his identity to my grave) snitched a small piece of pure sodium from Mr. Littlejohn's chemistry lab, which we placed in a baby food jar with some kerosene, and then took to the bridge over the Floyd River. We had heard that it was explosive on contact with water. We opened the jar and dumped the kerosene and sodium down to the river, about 20 feet below. The loud explosion startled me, and the ten foot high water flume that shot up into the air made me jump back.

Exploration of the outdoors was always a fascination. Another time, Bob Thews and I, working on Boy Scouting merit badges, hiked out to Fairacres and camped out in sleeping bags on the ground overnight in a copse of trees. We set up camp not too far from our swimming hole, started a camp fire, prepared and ate dinner, and then hit the sack shortly after dark. We awakened, and got up when we thought the sun was about to rise. We stoked up our campfire, and were ready to fix breakfast when a pickup truck pulled up to our campsite. Out stepped Dad, and queried, "How are you boys doing?" We said fine, and asked him the time as we had no watch. "10 o'clock," he replied to our astonishment. After he left, we went back to bed thinking about procuring a watch at the earliest opportunity.

Northwest Iowa and Southeastern South Dakota and northeastern Nebraska were richly fertile areas with fields, woods, streams, and rivers everywhere. The plains were chock-full of many animals, including mammals, fish, and birds. We especially enjoyed hunting for pheasants, since they were deeply ensconced in cornfields, bushes, and shrubs and they were also plentiful. They were also good to eat. Startled when we got within 10-20 feet of them hidden in the vegetation, they would jump up and flap their wings vigorously heading for the best escape route they could find. Bringing one down with a shotgun was no small task, and required good marksmanship.[34]

I learned that it is not a good idea to mess around with guns and ammunition. A couple of years before Mick was allowed to go hunting with Dad, he experimented with a .22 caliber cartridge by putting it in a vise, and then hitting it with a hammer. Not a brainy move I know, but he found that out himself the hard way. The cartridge exploded in all directions, and the projectile ricocheted off the garage concrete floor, hit the wall, bounced upward, hitting the ceiling, and then sprang down to hit Mick in the cheek. He bled like crazy, but other than a small scar near his dimple (that he had until the day he died), he was fine. Fine, and I'm sure a little wiser.

Two vivid hunting memories have remained with me all of my life. The first incident was when I shot a rabbit while out hunting with Dad. I was ordered to gut and skin it in the field to take home for a meal. Until that moment, I actually never thought about eating it. I just took some perverse measure of joy shooting it as it scooted away from me in the snow. Dad chastised me, and said, "We don't shoot anything we

---

[34] In those days, guns and ammo were easily accessible, but they were tools of provision – that is, we used the firearms to procure food for the table.

don't plan to eat." Those words, the noise the rabbit made when hit – an excruciatingly loud squeal – and having to take it home to eat, made Dad's lesson sink in. Every time I had rabbit after that, all I could think of was that screaming rabbit. It was as if my taste buds were at war with my memories.

The second, and scary, incident imbedded a very important lesson in gun safety when Dad, Gramps, my brother, Mick, and I were hunting pheasant in South Dakota. The routine was simple. We would line up along one edge of a corn field about 10 yards apart, and move in an echelon line abreast together across the field. When a bird jumped up, the closest person shot first. All of a sudden, Mick's shotgun went off without warning. I saw in an instant that the blast missed Dad's face by inches. My Dad felt the heat of the blast and was temporarily deafened by the report. It took a few seconds for it to sink in – the shot missed his face by inches. Mick had almost shot Dad! Dad got weak in the knees and couldn't speak, and Mick who was about 14 years old, began to cry. I think both Gramps and I almost wet our pants.

When all settled down, Mick explained through tears that the single shot 20 gauge shotgun he was carrying was difficult to cock and shoot. So he decided to shorten the process by cocking his shotgun and holding it ready to fire while walking through the field. Not a good plan, and my trepidation and fear since that time about where guns are pointed in my presence almost reach violent proportions when someone is acting carelessly. Dad had vigorously taught me to never to point a gun at a living thing that I don't plan to kill. I have never forgotten the lesson.

IV:

Progression:
Thrift, hardship, and contentment

*"Seek not greater wealth, but simpler pleasure;
not higher fortune, but deeper felicity."*
— Mahatma Gandhi

Modest economic levels in Leeds were basically little noticed by those of us growing up in Leeds. I don't remember very many families in Leeds that were families of means, except maybe the Rasmussens. The Rasmussen's dad had an animal pharmaceutical business on Floyd Avenue — so we thought they were wealthy whether they were or not. If they were, they sure didn't act any differently than the rest of us. However, most of us would have characterized Leeds as a robust "Blue Collar" community with hard-working, God-fearing people. It was a wonderful community in which to grow up and live.

Medical needs of Leeds were handled by the town doctors, who included Dr. Blackstone and Dr. Wiedemeyer, whose offices were next door to the fire station on Floyd Avenue across from Watt's Market. Dr. Blackstone's son, Byron, was involved in one of the most horrifying events known to us in the history of Leeds. When I was 18, Byron Blackstone, who was riding in a 1955 Corvette driven by his friend, hit a tree off Highway 75 (near Cole's Addition in Sioux City) going an estimated 100 miles per hour, decapitating the driver and throwing Byron a huge distance, killing him too.

Sioux City Journal Article: Byron Blackstone 1957

One thing I heard later about the driver was that he had several traffic violations before the accident, and his suspended license had just been reinstated the day before. Unquestionably, this was a huge tragedy, and a real life lesson for most of us who would have loved to have had that Corvette – it was a powerful deterrent to me as I was mastering the art of driving. Even after many decades, I never fail to think about Byron's death whenever I see a Corvette.

As I said, most of the families in Leeds were working, blue-collar types: construction workers (like my Dad, Granddad, and a Great Uncle), truck drivers, railroad employees, salesmen, store owners and employees, factory workers, and agricultural workers with some farmers living in or near the edge of town. Few of the families had both parents outside the home working in those days. In my case, I never can remember coming home from elementary school and not finding my Mom busily working in the home. Economic status meant very little to us then, since no one seemed to be ostensibly well to do in Leeds. I do remember that my mother was well pleased, when Dad came home after finding a new job that paid $60 a week, at the Fruehauf Company, which manufactured semi-truck trailers. Kent McCuddin, another family friend, also worked there so Dad was pleased about that too.

For my own economic needs, I remember asking my Dad for an allowance. He asked, "How much?" I hem-hawed around and softly offered, "15 cents a week?" He laughed. I was crushed. Sometimes he could deflate me without a word. Needless to say, I didn't get the allowance. I don't remember missing it since I got my own paper route shortly thereafter – introducing me to economic independence, even if limited in scope. If all of my customers on Tyler and Central Streets paid their bills on time, I could make about $1.25 a week. Plenty enough to buy a bicycle later on.

Our neighbor on the south of our home lived Beverly Pilotte, a member of the spring 1957 class and step-daughter of a police captain in Sioux City – Frank O'Keefe – definitely one of the ideal models of an Irish lawman. That distinguished him a lot in my eyes because I knew that he owned guns! What an image of a champion to a young kid. He even showed me his .38 caliber, 2-shot derringer once, which he carried in a holster inside his sock. I was immensely impressed. Not so impressed that I didn't misbehave once only for him to chastise me for shooting BB's at a couple of sparrows in the trees in his back yard. Frank though, has always been my idea of what a cop should be – he was gentle but strongly authoritative and firmly persuasive. The last thing I ever wanted was a report from Frank to my Dad that I had made trouble. Frank's example of consistent integrity was just one of many disincentives for me to avoid a life of misdemeanors and misconduct.

JOINING THE WORLD OF WORK
AND FINANCIAL INDEPENDENCE

When I was seven years old, and after Dad had returned from the war, Mick and I found some money that Dad had tucked away in a box in his bedroom closet. We took a bunch of the coins to the Crescent Park drug store, which used to be on the Northwest corner of 26th and Myrtle Streets, to buy some ice cream cones. We ordered the cones, and handed the money to the druggist, who laughed and told us it was worthless Japanese money and it was no good in his store. That was an abrupt introduction to what money really was. The druggist was undeniably no enabler and he crushed our aspirations for a cold ice cream cone.

Later on, I discovered that there were ways to accumulate some measure of affluence by working for money. The very first job I remember was working at for money earned me a big 15¢ an hour. I worked at a golf driving range near Prairie Creek (on the east side of the Crescent Park area by what is now called Hamilton Boulevard) gathering golf balls after the golfers had finished. Our low-tech approach was to use a bucket and a stick with a tin can affixed to the end of it to scoop up the balls and drop them in the bucket. Some years later, our jobs fell to mechanized tractors pulling a wide wire dragging box. This first job wasn't exciting, but in those days 5¢ would buy a Cherry Bing candy bar[35] (my favorite for the past seven decades), a cherry Coca-Cola (or other flavor you wished), and a box of Milk Duds! Fifteen cents went a long way back then.

---

[35] The Cherry Bing candy bar remains one of my favorites even today. They were made by the Palmer Candy Company, which still operates in the near west side of Sioux City's downtown area.

My Favorite Candy Bar – Palmer's Cherry Bing

I had many lessons yet to learn about using the meager money I earned. Like most kids, I usually spent my money on candy or soda (pop)[36], but I was to learn much about responsibility with money.

From there, I became eager to work for compensation wherever a kid, with transportation limited to a bicycle could find remuneration. I worked as a caddy at the Sioux City County Club, where caddies earned 5¢ per hole carrying a golfer's bag of clubs, plus tips. Usually, I did this after school for what the club called "twilight golf," which started about 4 pm and could go to dark. Most golfers tipped us three extra holes, so we almost always got 60¢ for a nine-hole round and double that for an 18 hole round. Getting this job required occasional physical prowess by getting and keeping my name on the caddie rotation list. Other kids often wanted to jump the line, which was first come, first served. A couple of times, I met the challenge to keep my

---

[36] In Iowa, carbonated beverages in bottles (and later cans) were called "pop." It wasn't until I travelled out of Iowa that I learned that in most places, those drinks are called soda. However, the term "soda" was confusing to me at first, because I had learned the term differently. A soda was a drink obtained at Wilkins Drug Store in a large glass, comprised of a scoop of ice cream, a squirt of flavored syrup, and filled to the brim with unflavored carbonated water.

spot in the line with some physical challenges and surviving a "contest of masculinity." It wasn't the first time that I was grateful for my above average stature.

Of course, I was in northwest Iowa, where snow came early and stayed late. On top of that winter temperatures could be brutal. My birthday is November 11, and from my earliest memory until I graduated from high school, I only remember one birthday when there was no snow on the ground. Winter seemed to hang around, sometimes until May. The upside of this was that I had many opportunities to shovel the snow off people's walks, driveways, and porches during the long winters, and that would earn about 50¢ a house, and sometimes more.

Another job I mentioned earlier and laden with grime was with my friend Bob Harward at Burke's Lumber and Coal. We unloaded coal from box cars on the railroad siding behind the lumber yard. It was hot, sweaty, and dirty work as I recall. This was one of those jobs replaced by machines later in my life. Once the skid loader came on the scene, manual labor for unloading box cars, or similar work, came to an end.

Example of a Skid Steer Loader That Replaced Many Laborers

I had another dirty, but pleasant, job in Wisconsin during the summer of 1953. I was 14, and my folks put me on a train to Minneapolis with a transfer to another train headed to Eau Claire, Wisconsin, where my Mom's sister, my Aunt Clarice,[37] picked me up and transported me to her home in Mondovi, Wisconsin. I loved the town of Mondovi, where they lived. Their home was huge, and had an innovation I'd never seen – a dining table with a built-in "lazy Susan" in the middle. It was perfect for their large family including my cousins, Colleen, Steve, Roy and Marilyn (Mimi). Across the street from their house was a small lake, with a water wheel at the outlet, which I think was used for grinding grain generations before. It was great for rowing, fishing, and exploring. I have wonderful memories of my times with the Ryans/Tanners, and my fondness for all of them continues unabated to today.

During that summer, I was lucky to get a temporary job working for a farmer east of town, helping put up (harvest and store) hay bales for his dairy herd. It was hot and dry work – lifting and loading hay bales on wagons, and getting them up to the second-story hay mow of the barn. My favorite part of this job was around noon when the farmer's wife brought out "dinner" for the guys on our work crew, it was a glorious and bountiful meal which I still savor in my mind six decades later. The homegrown fried chicken and home cured ham, homemade bread, homemade butter, homemade pies or cake, fresh sweet corn and beefsteak tomatoes, and other goodies were all produced on the farm. At 14 years of age, I ate until I thought I would burst. I don't remember how much or even if I was paid for my work. The heavenly food, lovingly prepared, and sufficient to satisfy any immense hunger was enough. I hated for that summer job to end. When I got back

---

[37] Aunt Clarice was Mom's older sister, and she introduced me to the concept of divorce, since she had divorced her first husband, John Ryan, after cousins Colleen (Mary Catherine) and Steve were born. She remarried a wonderfully pleasant man, John Tanner, who took her to Wisconsin where they had two more children, Roy and Marilyn (we all called her Mimi). Divorce was rare in those days, but I learned that in some deplorable situations it was justified.

home to Iowa, thanks to my Aunt Clarice, I think I had grown four inches and gained 20 pounds.

Not long after that, I started working in construction for my Dad and Granddad, whom I called Gramps. They were home builders, and worked for U.S. Homes, out of Des Moines. I worked for them building houses in Storm Lake, Sioux City, Missouri Valley, Omaha, and even Winner, South Dakota over a six year period during summers and holiday periods. The work was hard, but I learned a lot. I learned mainly that if I didn't go to college, I would have to <u>work</u> (maybe even suffer) for a living.

There is nothing more challenging than working in construction outdoors during the hot and humid summers and in the cold and bleak winters. During my Christmas vacations, I still get chills of cold when I remember going to the job early in the morning when the weather was 20° below zero, and the wind was blowing about 20 miles an hour, and snow was about a foot deep in Sioux City. It was miserable and a major reason I didn't follow my Dad and Grandad into the construction trade. I did develop a deep, abiding respect for the hard work my Dad and Gramps endured in order to put food on our table. They were tough stock, and I'll never lose my high regard for their endurance and perseverance, but it wasn't the kind of work I wanted to do.

It wasn't always tedious working with Dad and Gramps. Gramps had a great sense of humor which lightened the burden considerably. Once we were nailing cedar siding on a house in Kelly Park (southeast Sioux City), and I noticed that he made a big production about some nails. He would grumble, and then put the nail back into his overalls' apron. He said, "Some of these nails have their head on the wrong end and I should throw them away, but I'm saving them for the other side of the house." Then he would silently grin and go back to nailing. I would roll on the ground in laughter at his subtle humor.

Another time, I was working with Gramps on a job in Morningside, and at the end of the day, we had just put up a stud partition when it was quitting time. Gramps started gathering up his tools, and cleverly observed that "If we'd done that stud wall first, we'd have been done a long time ago." His humor was so understated and dry, that it didn't always register right away, but later it was hilarious. He also gave me advice to "look for a job where the clock was 10 minutes slow in the morning, and 10 minutes fast at the end of the day." What a guy.

Dad, on the other hand, was all about work. He demanded that we show up at the job site at least ½ hour before starting time to get tools out and set up so we could be working on the dot when the starting bell rang usually at 8 am. Once he had me nailing the 3rd nail in floor sheathing shiplap boards.[38] Dad and Gramps would lay the boards side by side and nail one nail per floor joist on each edge. My job was to put the third nail through the shiplap to the joist between the two other nails. It was difficult, because it required me to work on my knees. I got a bright idea to use a small wood platform with two of my old roller skates under it so I could scoot with my butt on the platform and then nail between my legs. It was much faster, and saved wear and tear on my legs. Inexplicably, when Dad saw the innovation, he angrily told me to "Quit screwing around and nail those boards like a man." Of course, I never challenged Dad, so I complied with some feelings of puzzlement. In retrospect, I don't think Dad connected work with fun or joy – more's the pity.

Work for Dad was an ethical commitment, not just a job. One morning, after working for Dahl's Trucking as a diesel mechanic for a few

---

[38] Shiplap was sub-floor sheathing was made of pine or fir, and the boards were generally available in 6-inch or 8-inch widths. They ran from 8-foot to 18-foot lengths, and their long edges were rabbeted with a ½ inch open channel along one edge. The boards fit together along their long edge and required two or three nails. They are seldom used today, since the advent of cheaper particle board sheets of 4' x 8'.

years after he had lost his eye, he was laid off. We never knew about the job loss, because Dad left their office, and immediately "hit the bricks" looking for work. After pounding the pavement for several hours, he was hired that very afternoon at Fruehauf Trailer Corporation to help build semi-truck trailers. It was as if he could not have come home without a job. We all slept better knowing the security of Dad's commitment to work.

There were other similar incidents and I learned that work to Dad was serious business. He was formidably tenacious when trying to get a job done. That's just the way he was. His example of hard – I mean really hard – work set me on the straight path to independence and self-reliance. Boasting was vigorously scorned, but self-accountability for doing a good job was highly esteemed. Dad's lessons about work became imbedded in my bones. I will share some more thoughts about these experiences later on.

Work, in and of itself, can be very educational. In modern times, work assignments in real jobs are a part of the school curriculum – officially that is. In my youth, work was something you did of economic necessity while getting a formal education. That continued for me all the way through high school, and three college degrees.

One of the most onerous jobs was after the 1953 flood in Leeds (see page 61) when Bob Harward and I, along with a couple of other guys, helped Dick Watt's dad clean out the mud from his grocery on Floyd Avenue, across from the fire station. Shoveling mud was not only ugly work, it was dangerous. We had to get inoculations for typhoid fever at the fire station because we were working with smelly, slimy mud that contained all manner of toxic waste, including raw sewage. We also cleaned the can goods in buckets of water, until Mr. Watt sorrowfully found out that the Health Department prohibited sale of anything that had been inundated by the flood waters. His economic loss was staggering.

A job I enjoyed was helping pick a cornfield for Tom Porsch's dad, Darrel. His cornfield was north of 46th Street, and east of a dirt road that later became an extension of Tyler Street, and we picked the entire field by hand. Striding through the corn rows, chock-full of spiny cockle burrs that stuck to everything including skin, we picked ears of corn, and tossed them over our heads into a wagon with a tall backboard on the opposite side. The wagon was pulled by a horse that never went faster than a speed with which we could keep up. It took a long time to fill that wagon, but the warm fall weather, cloudless blue skies, and cool breezes are what I remember of the experience.

Of course, like lots of kids my age, I had a paper route for the Sioux City Journal on Central, Tyler, and Polk Streets and made a steady income of about $1.25 a week. That was a fortune to a 12 year old kid. Jobs like that were easy to come by, but difficult to stay with during the winter months. Fortunately, my Dad would take pity on me if we had bitterly cold temperatures or blinding snow storms, and drive me around my route in his pickup truck.

In the summer of 1950, I worked on the golf course at the Sioux City Boat Club (now Two Rivers Golf Club). I served as a groundskeeper on the 16th green during the first Sioux City Open Golf Tournament. The Open drew a lot of big name golfers to Sioux City, including Jack Burke, Porky Oliver, and most notable of all – Sam Snead. Jack Burke won the tournament and was awarded $2,600. That was more money that I could wrap my young mind around. My job was to repair "dents" in the greens, when a golfer hit an approach shot that caused a divot in the green. I used a dinner fork to fluff the hole or dent up and back into shape so it wouldn't unnecessarily affect the path of a putted ball. That job paid 75¢ an hour. Big bucks for 12 year old kids in those days. One memory I have during that time was when Porky Oliver missed a key putt, and kicked his putter about 20 feet into the air. Midway in the putter's flight, it split in two. Porky had to putt the remaining two greens with one of his irons.

Sometimes I worked for free. Once I got up at "zero dark hundred" and accompanied Bob Harward's dad, Ed, on his rural milk route, which he had to do seven days a week – no misses allowed. We traveled all around the country surrounding Sioux City to the southeast, stopping at farms along the way, and picking up 10 gallon cans of fresh milk. The cans were then transported to Roberts' Dairy, where they were tested, weighed, and dumped into the bulk containers. The cans were then steam washed, and put back into the truck ready for the next day. This was another one of those jobs that convinced me that I didn't want to do that sort of thing. I did enjoy working with Ed though. He was an ebullient man who always uplifted my spirits, and a close friend of Dad's.

Another time, I worked at Vennard's Nursery, northeast of Leeds, where gladioluses were grown on a 20 acre spread. Jim Brehm, another friend, was the supervisor – or straw boss.[39] The gladiolus bulbs had to be planted in the spring and dug up in the fall to be stored in a warehouse over the winter. There were hundreds of species, and the colors spanned the rainbow many times over. The nursery also raised Austrian pines, which were sold to homeowners. One of the most onerous jobs we did there was plant 50 of those pine trees (all about 4' tall) at the home of a member of the Cannon Family (of towel fame I think) out near the Country Club on North Hamilton in Sioux City. That job took some serious energy, a good measure of time, and hefty exper-

Austrian Pine Tree
(Pinus Nigra)

---

[39] Jim, at that early age, showed potential of becoming an effective ramrod for a crew, which he fulfilled in his adult life as an electrical grid repair supervisor with a large workforce in the Midwest.

tise and skill in wielding a round point shovel in Loess clay.

My labors were rewarded with wages that might seem meager today, but larger rewards I gained in the way of experience were beneficial. Dad and Gramps always set excellent examples for me in work, and neither one of them ever shied away from physical labor. In fact, Gramps was up on a ladder working on a remodel project when he suffered a heart attack at age 79. Driving himself to the hospital, he died about a week later. Dad worked until he was 80 years old before retiring. He lived to age 93. They were both living examples that hard work is not detrimental.

V.

Home: Relationships, people who matter and places that never leave you

"Home is the nicest word there is." — <u>Laura Ingalls Wilder</u>

We lived in two different homes in Leeds – first at 4332 Tyler Street (built 1900) from 1940 until 1943 when Dad joined the Marines and left for the South Pacific to fight the Japanese. We lived there for a while after he departed for the war, but soon moved out to Crescent Park. I had finished Kindergarten and my first semester of first grade at Hawthorne School, and completed the rest of first grade, all of second grade, and the first semester of third grade at Crescent Park.

Me at age 18 months in Beresford, SD

L to R: Grandma, Neil Jr., Me (in front), Mom, Karen, and Grandpa – all Postons)

Me at age 3 in Leeds (On Tyler Street)

After WWII, Dad used his GI Bill in 1946 to purchase our second home in Leeds at 4548 Central Avenue (built 1910). I always thought we had loads of room in those homes, but the Tyler St. home only had 1100 square feet and the Central St. home had less than 1300 square feet of living space. They were remarkably small by today's standards, but to me as a kid, they were huge. We even had lots of hiding places – the basement with only an outside entrance and a basement room not unlike a root cellar with brick walls, the attic with a crawl space accessible through a cubby hole in our second-floor bedroom, and the closet under the stairs on the north side of the dining room accessible only from my folks' bedroom.[40] The Central Street home seemed much more spacious and pleasant, since it was two stories.

We lived in the Tyler Street home from my earliest memory of a house until August, 1943, when we moved to Crescent Park on the west side of Sioux City (2719 George Street) to be near to my Irish Grandmother (Cathryn Irene Flanagan Schultz) for the duration of the war. About six months after Dad returned from the war (see page 27) on Christmas Eve, 1945, we moved back to Leeds. We moved to our new domicile at 4548 Central Avenue, on the southeast corner of 46th Street, which was a clay dirt road and still is today. Central Avenue was paved, but it ended in front of our house. At least the paved part did, but the unpaved road continued on up the hill past the Pettit's and Yockeys' home to end at the Wren Philpott farm.

The lot for our Central Street house was dug out of the clay hill east of the house, but we needed a more level yard, and a driveway behind the house where Dad planned to build a garage. I was amazed at the

---

[40] Remembering that home as large when it wasn't reminds me of the cartoon of a man dragging his young son through snow up to the boy's chest. The father, looking unwaveringly ahead and striding forward in mid-calf deep snow, saying, "This is nothing – when I was your age, the snow was chest deep!" I guess the perceived size of surroundings is directly proportional to your own size.

Horse-drawn, Man Operated Dirt Scraper/Scoop

contraction Dad used to grade the yard and create the driveway from 46th Street, which was actually pulled by a horse. It was a "dirt scraper/scoop" pulled by a horse connected to the eye bolt at the front, and manned by a man holding the handle at the back. As the horse pulled, the operator lifted the back of the scoop so it would bite in to the dirt. Once the scoop was full, the operator lowered the bar at the back and the front of the scoop lifted off the ground. The horse then pulled the scoop where the dirt was to go, and the operator simply lifted the handle at the back quickly, so the scoop would empty upside down as the horse moved forward. Dad dug a driveway out of the yellow clay bank, which left a six foot tall embankment to the east and about 12 feet of driveway width south to the southeast corner of our lot, where the garage was to go.

The excess dirt was hauled to the north yard, which was lower than the rest of the yard, and dumped. Eventually, the entire lot, except for the steep bank on the Central Avenue frontage, was relatively level, giving us a good place to play games and run around.

With the new driveway, leveled side yard, and planned garage all accomplished in the summer of 1947, Dad launched the first of dozens of remodeling projects to our home, which in my mind seemed eternally under renovation and never completed. Dad enjoyed tearing into a place in the home, and transforming it into something better.

Our "new" house had two stories, with a living room, dining room, bedroom, bathroom, and kitchen on the first floor, and two bedrooms upstairs on the second floor. There was no basement, except for a "root cellar" accessible from an outside entrance behind our house.

Thanks to the GI Bill, which provided low cost loans to veterans to purchase a home, it was the first home my parents actually owned.

The dirt road, 46th Street, was of typical construction in that area at that time. It was clay dirt (and still is), no gravel, no oil, and unique to a fault. All of Leeds, in fact all of Sioux City, sits upon huge compacted and eroded dunes of finely pulverized and powdered clay soil left behind by the Glaciers some 250 centuries ago.[41] The dirt roads and our driveway, which entered our lot from 46th street, were made of Loess clay, which was as sloppy, sticky, and slippery as it could be when wet, but hard as a brick when bone dry. It wasn't hard to get stuck in that stuff after a rain and it was impossible to dig a hole in it when dry. I always appreciated the hill location, and have favored living on hills my entire life since, mainly because of my experience in Leeds when the Floyd River flooded nearly the whole town on June 8, 1953, inundating everything in Leeds a few blocks below our hilltop perch.

1953 Leeds Flood – 41st and Floyd Avenue

---

[41] This clay soil is called "loess" or *Löss* – a German word defined as: *Löss oder Löß ist ein vom Wind transportiertes und auch vom Wind abgelagertes Sediment, das aus Feinmaterial – vor allem aus Schluff – besteht."* (Loess or loess is transported by wind and (is) wind-deposited sediment, which consists of fine material of mainly silt).

The flood was the most devastating experience imaginable for everyone in Leeds, especially for my grandparents who lived at 4220 Polk Street – just above Floyd Avenue which became popularized as "Flood" Avenue thereafter.

Leeds Residents Evacuating by Boat (Flood 1953)

Below is a picture of Gram and Gramps Poston's home at 4220 Polk Street, as the water was both rushing in and still rising. The water level eventually reached midway up their first floor windows before it began to recede.[42] Most everything in their home was destroyed and unusable after the water receded. Even more devastating, the onrushing flash flood waters hit the east side of their house with such force that the back basement wall caved in, destroying Gramps' elegant ShopSmith saw, construction equipment, and his basement woodshop.

---

[42] The 1953 flood by the Floyd River was attributed to approximately 15 inches of rain upstream in the Sheldon, Iowa area.

My Grandparents' Polk Street home under water in June, 1953

Our close friends, the Harwards, didn't fare much better. They lived on Harrison Street about half a block away from Floyd Avenue near the little Leeds Park west of the library, and as the flood water hit their neighborhood, Bob and Janice tried to move some of their furniture up to the second floor. Unfortunately, they could only get the living room couch halfway up the staircase. Their home was seriously damaged with several feet of water, and unfortunately the couch didn't escape the acrid, muddy flood waters.

My grandparents eventually lost their home due to the flood and insufficient insurance, and the Harwards relocated to higher ground. "Flood Avenue" was a name that went down in infamy for all of us who experienced the flood. Many people, especially the merchants, lost their homes and businesses. Floods are always destructive because of the massive and dreadful efforts required to clean up the abominable mess.

Floyd Avenue Merchants' Cleaning Up Flood Damage

To this day, having experienced flood and a devastating fire in 1983 that destroyed nearly everything we owned, I still feel that flood damage is the most destructive and pernicious calamity that can befall a family.

Rainfall wasn't the only tribulation that confronted Leeds. In the summer of 1946, we hadn't had any rain for nearly two months. Drought created conditions perfect for a prairie fire on the north and east of our house. We looked out the east kitchen window and witnessed the whole hill on fire. The speed with which it marched across the land was astounding. The entire hill burned to ashes in less than 30 minutes. Later, after Mom wondered what had caused the fire, I traced the burned area to 46th street where I found a burned cigarette by the side of the road. I thought the fire most likely started there.

Another setback came in May of 1947. When we woke up to 4 inches of snow and freezing temperatures, our apple tree up on the bank east of the garage lost every one of its blossoms. We didn't get a single apple that year.

Tornadoes, rain storms, and blizzards seemed commonplace in our area. Tornadoes were rumored to be unable to cross a river or a lake, but I found that to be false when a tornado tore eastward out of Nebraska across the Missouri River and hit the oxbow[43] Brown's Lake south of Sioux City, demolishing everything in its path. In winter, blizzards were infrequent, but I note to this day that I can only remember one birthday (November 11) in Leeds when there wasn't snow on the ground. Only one Christmas in my memory was without snow, when I could ride my bike. Snow, once on the ground, seemed to stay until spring.

We learned early on that warm, protective clothing was essential for personal survival, and the man-made fabrics were much less efficient than the natural fibers – wool, cotton, linen, down, etc. – especially wool, which was surprisingly warm even when wet.

Good Old Iowa Snow In Siouxland

I'm not sure of the year – probably a few years before I could drive (1954), snow was so deep that Dad fastened a red bandana at the top

---

[43] "Oxbow" refers to the main stream of a meandering river, which has cut across a narrow bend and no longer flows around the loop of the bend. The Missouri River historically changed its course many times and created many oxbow lakes.

of the car's radio antenna, to help other drivers see the car at intersections with snow drifts piled as high as the car. Peculiar as that may seem, I also remember some of Dad's pictures from his truck driving days from the Sioux City stockyards to the Black Hills in which he captured a photo of a train stuck in snow as high as the engineer's cab. I'm not impressed with some of the contemporary weather reporters that warn us of an impending "blizzard." The normal outcome of those hyped up forecasts usually is a normal, moderate snowfall with maybe a little wind – usually, not what we would call a blizzard in Leeds during the 1940's and 1950's.

Despite the adversity of climate, we had some memorable adventures in winter, which always seemed to arrive on or about my birthday (November 11) and usually ended in early April (except in 1947). People who live in northwestern Iowa lived by the adage, "If it doesn't kill you, it will make you stronger."[44] The four seasons arrived like clockwork every year, and weather was something one had to learn to handle or succumb to its often fickle and nasty nature.

"Killer" Snow Storm in Northwest Iowa

Snow was overwhelming at times during the winter, but somehow, we always survived and frequently enjoyed all seasons of the year. The hill behind our house provided one of the best snow sledding venues I've ever seen. Everyone had a sled, but it was more fun to borrow Dad's grain scoop shovel, point the handle downhill, plop your bottom into

---

[44] This axiom is generally true with respect to winter – upper Midwestern states (Minnesota, Wisconsin, North Dakota, Iowa, etc.) have life expectancy rates among the highest in the nation.

the shovel, lift your legs and take off. Funny — I don't remember being cold. I must have been, but memory doesn't store those feelings for some reason.

Winter was never dull in Leeds. After a brisk snowfall, which seemed to come more frequently then than it does today, sometimes the roads became snow packed due to the vehicle traffic. My friends and I, using our customary "ingenuity," would sneak up behind a Sioux City bus at a stop sign, squat down, grab the rear bumper, and keeping our feet underneath us, get pulled by the bus when it pulled ahead. It was great fun, until my mother heard from some meddlesome neighbor about our exploits. That stifled our creativity for a while at least.

Scooting along on an old American Flyer sled

Despite the many challenges of geography and climate, the social environment in Northwest Iowa was unusually safe and hospitable. We never locked our home or our car. We enjoyed the feeling of safety and security even while away from home. For example, one summer we all piled in the car and drove to Spirit Lake where we enjoyed a week in a rustic cabin on the shore. Returning home, I jumped out of the car and ran into the house to use the bathroom. The door to our house had been left unlocked as it always was whether we were there or not. Nothing had happened to our unlocked home all that time, and nothing had been disturbed. Oddly, we just took that for granted. The same was true of leaving keys in the car without any concern of theft or vandalism. Those are wonderful feelings – not commonly found in the contemporary world.

VI.

Family: Blessings, adversities, and lots of love

"Family — One of nature's masterpieces."
— <u>George Santayana</u>. *The Life of Reason*[45]

Sometimes, when I was in the mood to share, and my kids or grand-kids were willing to listen, I might talk about what it was really like to live in our Leeds homes. Some of my recollections are met with a look of disbelief — almost like my Irish heritage was creating exaggeration. No matter their incredulity — I too find much of my experience almost surreal and unbelievable. Nevertheless, despite the decades since, I still remember things that today might be considered preposterous.

Consider the fact that in our home on Tyler Street, my Mom used one of the kitchen windows on the north side of the house as a refrigerator. It was a two-pane, double-hung window, with a two panel storm window on the outside. Dad built a wooden platform with triangular sides to sit outside on the window ledge, with the storm window extended out at the bottom to enclose the space. Mom would open the inside double hung window, lifting the pane up, put things she wanted to cool or keep cold (in the cold months, which sometimes stretched interminably) on the platform, and close the inside window. It was makeshift and crude, but it worked.

While in that home, my brother Mick and I had a harrowing experi-

---

[45] Santayana, George. Retrieved from:
http://www.brainyquote.com/quotes/topics/topic_family.html. 25 November 2013.

ence that shaped our skepticism about food tasting forever. Mom had parked the car in our backyard just off the alley, and she told us to go out and get in the back seat of the car, which we did. I think I was about four or so, and Mick was about two. When we got in the back seat, we noted a jar on the seat with a white powder inside. Thinking it was sugar, we opened the jar and took a pinch of the powder and put it in our mouths. We soon regretted that decision.

What I remember next is hazy, but I remember a sudden excruciating pain in my mouth, as did Mick, and we ran screaming into the house. Mom took us outside and rinsed our mouth out with a garden hose, several times, while admonishing us repeatedly for getting into something we had no business getting into. The powder was lye, or sodium hydroxide, which is highly toxic and often used as a drain cleaner. Mom was using it to make soap. Lye, along with lard and a little vinegar, is one of the ingredients for soap making. In those days, it was cheaper to make soap than it was to buy it. Mom needn't have admonished us – we learned the lesson the hard way!

In June of 1944, I completed the first semester of kindergarten (after enrolling in January),[46] Dad had enlisted in the United States Marine Corps, and he left for the war with Japan the previous summer. That month, to cut costs and have family nearby, Mom moved us to Crescent Park near my Grandmother (Flanagan) Schultz. I remember having a lot of fun in Crescent Park, especially since our house on George Street had a front porch about 4' above the yard, and we could play underneath it, digging and constructing elaborate play "towns" with cardboard houses and plastic toy people. We had a different venue to explore all the time we lived there.

---

[46] Kindergarten enrollment at Hawthorne Elementary (K-6) required a child to be five years of age before beginning. Since my birthday was in November, I missed the September enrollment, but started in January (second semester) since I was then five. The "mid-year" enrollment pattern was discontinued years ago, and I doubt if it will ever be resurrected.

While Dad was gone during the war, Mom gathered the three of us together for a family picture – circa 1945. Since Dad didn't return until December 24, 1945, Mom had the picture taken to send to him overseas. I'm sure it gave him inspiration for what he was fighting for.

Poston Family (Dad was in the South Pacific) in 1945

In 1943, before Dad embarked for the south Pacific, Mom took the train to California to spend some time with Dad and Ed and Toots Harward, who were living in southern California where Ed was serving in the US Army. Dad came up from the Marine base at Miramar (then north of San Diego, now surrounded by the metro area). It was a surreal scene, with Dad soon to leave for parts and a future unknown in the war. Communication was unbelievably difficult during those days with millions of men overseas fighting battles in both hemispheres.

Letters would often take a couple of months to go back and forth, and telephonic or video communication was either impossible or not invented at the time. However, a small miracle occurred when Mom went to a movie.

Mom and Dad in California before
Dad shipped out during WWII

In the fall of 1944, Mom and Dad's sister, Dorothy, caught a double feature movie at a theater in Beresford, South Dakota, where Grandma and Grandpa Poston lived. Mom and Dorothy were surprised to see what they thought was my Dad in a *Movietone* newsreel which showed film footage of the Marines on Saipan in June of 1944. They were sure it was Dad, so they sat through both movies again, and watched the newsreel a second time. Even more convinced it was Dad, they went to the theater manager who stopped the movie and played the newsreel a couple of times.

The film clip showed Dad – with a rifle strapped to his shoulder — escorting a group of civilian Japanese women and children, and carrying a Japanese child of about 18 months of age. Mom wrote to Dad asking him about it, but it took three months for his reply to come back. He stated that he did remember something like that, but it was apparently not something out of the ordinary.

My Dad, Ken (who went by his [and my] middle name) declined to talk to me or my brother about the war after he returned. We knew he had been a Marine on Saipan, Peleliu, and Iwo Jima – all three places had huge losses of Marines with horrific battles[47] – but he would only say, "You don't want to hear about it" when asked. Our curiosity was always high, because we knew it had to be ugly judging from the mementos Dad brought home from the South Pacific war with Japan, including a Japanese rifle, Japanese money and coins, wedding rings, and a rising sun flag. It had to be a grim experience that was too painful to think about after returning home.

Incredibly, in 2012, when I obtained a video of Dad while he served on Saipan, it was a brief glimpse, but there he was, carrying a Japanese child that the Marines had removed from a cave just like Mom had described it. The video glimpse was first viewed almost happenstance on the *Military Channel* and I luckily recorded it on my Digital Video Recorder, courtesy of Dish Network. Later I found the same video in a Reader's Digest DVD. I was so grateful that Mom had shared the story with me when I was very young. I sent a copy of the video to each of Dad's grandchildren, some of my cousins, and my sister, my only surviving sibling.

---

[47] On Iwo Jima alone, the Marines lost 7000 men in the five week battle, about 200 men a day, and the Japanese lost about 22,000 soldiers. The battle for Saipan cost 3500 American Marines their lives and the battle for Peleliu took another 1500 Marine lives. . It was a very high price to pay for small amounts of real estate.

I think it very fortuitous that we have the movie excerpt due to providence and my fondness for historical military films. Below is a screen shot of the *Movietone* video I saw of my Marine dad – one chance in a million[48]

WWII Photo of Dad on Saipan, Marianas Islands, July, 1944

Dad was gone for nearly three years, so I was seven when he came home on Christmas Eve, 1945. When he entered the house, I was scared of this giant of a man in his dress green Marine uniform as he entered the door. The fear abated quickly as I learned immediately that this was my Dad. Of course, Mick and I wanted to hear all about the war – we had been playing war a lot at that age – but Dad never

---

[48] Screenshot from *Victory in the Pacific 1944-1945*. Disc 3: *Reader's Digest WWII in the Pacific*. Questar, Chicago, IL. (2010).

talked to me or my brother about it. I think that memories had to be horrendous for veterans, and my Dad tucked the dreadfulness and horror away in a compartment of things he wanted to forget.

Ironically, in 2005 – 60 years after the war — Dad finally opened up about his wartime experiences to my eight year old grandson, Alex, who had been asked to interview a member of the military and write up the story for his English class. It was truly a surprise, and a gift for posterity that we learned about his time in the most terrible war in history.

Pot-bellied Stove,
circa 1946

After the war, in 1946, we moved into our Central Avenue house in Leeds, where I re-entered Hawthorne School in third grade (first semester). The heat for our entire two-story house was a pot-bellied stove located in the center of the ground floor "dining" room – today it would be called a family room – albeit a modestly-sized one). The stove burned wood when we had it on hand. When we didn't have wood, we burned mostly coal, which we had to buy and store in a coal shed attached to the house adjacent to the east end of the back porch. Coal came in bulk form, requiring a bucket and a shovel to transport into the house.

The hard part of the whole routine was carrying the coal into the house, through the kitchen, and then placing it into the stove without spilling it. A few years later, we happily had a different type of coal. The coal was compressed into "bricks" about 4" high, 10" wide and 15" long, and then wrapped and sealed with brown paper. Those bricks were immeasurably cleaner than ordinary bulk coal, and much easier to carry into the house. We got the coal bricks from Burke Lumber and Coal on Floyd Avenue.

Fuel hadn't been a problem. Since Dad was a carpenter in those days, he had access to huge supplies of discarded construction job wood scraps and trash, consisting of cutoffs and unusable boards. He would cut it all up into bite-size chunks for use in the stove. It worked fine, but burned very hot and didn't have the staying power of coal, making it more work to keep the stove supplied with fuel. One memory I have of that stove is that it often would glow a bright red when burning a fresh load of fuel. It was like we had a night light, when we needed to come down the stairs to the only bathroom in the house.

Moreover, after the fuel in the stove burned down, whether coal or wood, we had to scoop out the cinders (we called them "clinkers") carefully so as to not raise any dust, place them in the bucket, which was oval at the top, and then dispose of them outdoors. That was the easy part – the cinders and ashes made great artificial paving for our clay dirt driveway. The cast iron teapot on top emitted steam to hydrate the house during winter season. The upstairs was heated by means of a register[49], about 12" square, located in the dining room ceiling and in the floor of our bedroom upstairs. Mick and I used to tussle over who got to stand on the register on cold mornings while we dressed. Our old double bed was blessed with a heavy, hand-made quilt of 3 or 4 layers of wool between sewn pieces of cotton material. I remember it to be heavy, very confining, but very warm.

I also remember that our bedroom windows frosted over in early No-

---

[49] Floor registers, or heat registers, were metal grates, set flush with the floor that allows the passage of heated air from a source down below. In our case, the register was right in the middle of our room, directly above the pot-bellied stove.

vember and stayed that way until mid to late March, and if you wanted to see outdoors, you had to blow on the window with your warm breath to create a "peep hole." I don't remember it being cold, but I'm sure it was. We were just acclimated to it. Later in life, when living in California, Arizona, Oklahoma, and Montana, that body adjustment phenomenon was very useful. I've seen how the versatility of the human body allows us to adjust to excruciatingly hot deserts or intolerably freezing snow and ice-bound areas, and the human body's adaptability never fails to amaze me.

Living upstairs was an advantage in winter, when the heat from the first floor would come up the staircase at the north end of the dining room. I do remember one problem with those stairs. A couple of the stair treads "squeaked" when we went up or down the staircase, and Mom or Dad would always hear us going up or down no matter the time of night. I was never able to sneak up the stairs after spending too much time outdoors with friends in the evenings.

At some point around 1947, Mom took me, Brother Mick and Sister Lynda to a photographer to have our picture taken. On Mom and Dad's 25th anniversary in 1963, I had the photo re-created in charcoal by an artist friend in Arizona, Steve Laney, and it remains one of my fondest depictions of the three of us. It now hangs in the home of my brother's son, Douglas Poston, in Riverside, California.

Bill, Mick, and Lynda Poston, 1947

Of note was that clothing we wore in the 1940's and 1950's was not made of manmade material. The natural fibers of wool, cotton, linen, and down made up our wardrobe. Mostly, boys wore "Levi's" – blue denim material – very hardy and durable. We bought them without understanding inseam length, so most of us rolled up the bottom of pants legs. In warm times, we wore T-shirts, or went bare back. Sneakers were the choice of shoe, but leather shoes were de rigeur for school and church. Today in Iowa we occasionally see a woman wearing a "burka" head covering, which is reminiscent of the head scarves that girls and women wore 60 years ago.

I recall my favorite coat for winter – a bulky, thick woolen hip-length coat, red and green plaid, called a Mackinac (pronounced mak'-in-aw)[50]. Wet or dry, it was always warm. Winter foot wear required "overshoes" – rubber boots that pulled over our shoes – which zipped or buckled up. Keeping dry was half the battle in keeping warm during the many days below freezing in Northwest Iowa.

Dress was informal, more due to our modest economic status rather than a conscious choice of fashion. We did dress up for special occasions and church, with "dress pants," which were usually woolen pants. Other times we wore what were then called "dungarees" but are now generically called "jeans." We wore a sweater on occasion when needed.

Heating and cooling were much more primitive in those days, much more than found in the average home today. During the sixth grade, I walked home one cold winter day after school and entered the enclosed back porch as usual. I was immediately taken aback because the porch was almost warm. That had never happened before. I took

---

[50] The coat is named after Mackinac Island, which sits in the Straits of Mackinac at the point where Lake Huron joins with Lake Michigan and Michigan's Upper and Lower Peninsulas.

off my rubber boots and coat, entered the kitchen, and was overpow-ered by the warmth and heat reaching from the dining room to the back door. I quickly saw that the pot-bellied stove was gone! In its place, I saw a smaller, modern looking dark brown stove that had two burners that used fuel oil instead of coal. Wow! The difference in heat-ing that uninsulated barn of a house was amazing – not to mention less hassle in handling coal, wood, cinders and ashes. The new stove received its fuel through a line under the floor coming from a storage tank outside on the north side of the house under the box elder tree. The automaticity of this innovation intrigued me, and it has been val-ued ever since.

Air conditioning was literally and completely unknown in my experi-ence until after I was married. Our upstairs bedroom was poorly venti-lated. We could open the north and south windows and hope for a cooling breeze in summer, but when it was excruciatingly hot in our upstairs bedroom, Mick and I would open the west window in our sis-ter's room and step out on the roof above the front porch to sleep there. Usually, evenings on the prairie in summer were blessed with a light breeze, which helped make it cool enough to sleep, and if it was a stiff breeze, it helped to keep the mosquitoes at bay.

Mom should have been an inventor. When summer came, and it often was just as hot then as it was cold in the winter months, she opened the kitchen window of our home on Central Avenue, placed a large dishpan full of ice in front of the window on her kitchen counter, and then put a fan behind the ice but in front of the window so cool fresh air would flow from the outside into the house. Crude, but the me-chanical fundamentals were there. She was always inventive that way. Her little chuckle and cleverness at such times was pure delight. Her "evaporative cooler" was effective, if not attractive.

Baths in the mid-1940s consisted of water heated on the kitchen stove and poured into a large 2-bushel washtub on the kitchen floor in which all three kids took a bath. As the oldest, I got to go first. There were many disadvantages being the oldest sibling, but the bath routine wasn't one of them. We bathed regularly every Saturday night – whether we needed it or not. After we got a propane gas water heater about 1950, Dad installed a shower stall into the only bathroom in the house, where we previously had only a toilet and sink. By today's standards, it wasn't much, but very functional and convenient – except when my sister was in there for what seemed like hours during her junior high days.

Food preparation was another matter altogether. Cooking in the early days was a difficult undertaking, due to the inefficient cooking stoves. Mom had a simple oil-powered stove and oven until about 1950, when propane gas became available. That created several more improvements in our lives. When I was in ninth grade, we switched to a gas-fired furnace located in the basement with forced air vents and a gas water heater that held 40 gallons of water, providing luxurious extended showers. Also, Mom was able to create some culinary dishes with more baking and frying options available.

Some dishes weren't to my liking in those days, although I find that hard to describe because today I'll eat most everything without hesitation, except maybe cooked beets, which is understandable – at least in my opinion. If something was put on my plate though, regardless of who put it there, it was mandatory that it be eaten and completely eaten. Fortunately, our dog, Lucky stayed under the kitchen table during meals, and it was easy to slip him something that I didn't care for, like canned green beans that were boiled until they nearly became mush. Nonetheless, to escape eating them, I remember tossing Lucky a morsel of a green bean under the kitchen table. My toss was followed by my Dad then asking, "Bill – did you eat those beans?" I knew by the tone of his voice that I'd better tell the truth, so I confessed to slipping something to the dog. He said he knew that, because my toss to the dog had struck his knee first. Another lesson learned – if you're going to get rid of some mushy green beans, don't try to toss them to your dog without carefully aiming first.

Meals were usually predictable. With my Dad it was usually meat and potatoes as a rule, except when Mom's rule of no meat came every Friday.[51] We grew lots of potatoes on the vacant lot on the south side of our house, and that garden seemed to produce enough potatoes to supply the whole state of Iowa – or at least as I thought so after digging them up, bagging them in about a dozen 100-pound sacks and dragging them to our basement cellar under the house. We did give several sacks away to grandparents, other family, and friends.

Dad was so fond of potatoes in any form, that a meal wasn't a meal unless in included potatoes – boiled, mashed, fried, chopped, whole, baked, scalloped or even as chips. Speaking of chips, I will always remember that we could buy a small package of potato chips in the Leeds High lunchroom for 5 cents. The brand was a local one, no longer seen, named "Kitty Clover Potato Chips." We loved those things, but learned later in life that they were probably not good nutrition. Tasty just the same. Sad that the company folded in 1956.

Kitty Clover Potato Chip Tin Around 1954

---

[51] Catholics were prohibited from eating meat on Fridays in reparation for sin, so Mom would serve some acceptable alternative – macaroni and cheese casserole, tuna and rice casserole, potato soup, etc. On potato soup nights, it was a good practice to go to bed early, because by 10 o'clock, Mick and I knew we would be hungry again.

In point of fact, to this day, I rarely pass up a serving of potatoes when offered, but probably due to other reasons, i.e., nutrition, it may not be the best choice.[52]

Dad would enlist my and Mick's help in planting and harvesting our potatoes. It was "man's" work, which meant our younger sister got a free pass. In the spring, we would place cuts of potatoes (with an eye on each) in the furrows that he deftly carved into the clay soil. Then, nature was given charge of the crop, and we would harvest them in the fall with a garden spading fork with four tines. The fork would lift the potatoes out of the ground and leave the dirt behind. We then loaded the potatoes into burlap bags that held 100 pounds of potatoes. We would have what seemed like a dozen or more bags. Fortunately, Dad was the only one able to carry the potatoes to the cellar. When required to do it, Mick and I dragged the bags across the ground.

The cellar where we stored the potatoes was rather a grim place – small, dark and dingy with brick walls and a concrete floor. When we were little, Mick and I were startled out of our wits when we opened the basement door, located outside on the east side of the house outdoors, and discovered a huge python snake coiled on the top step looking at us menacingly. Actually, it was a little 18 inch garter snake, but when you're ten years old, and you have seen Johnny Weismuller as Tarzan wrestle a huge snake in vivid black and white movies at the Iowa Theater, and don't know much about reptiles, you are vulnerable

---

[52] My favorite form of potato is baked, with sour cream and chives. In January of 1957, our high school graduation banquet included a serving of baked potato. As usual, I ate the entire potato, including the skin (or jacket), with relish. Then I looked around the room and discovered that I was the only one present that ate the skin. Although I later learned that it is the skin of the potato that is the source of the best nutrients, it was uncomfortable being the only person to eat the whole thing. Fortunately, I got over it and still eat the whole baked potato and I truly enjoy it!

to terror in such circumstances. We nearly wet our britches. We never saw that snake again, but we never opened that door without making sure it wasn't waiting for us.

Despite the snake hazards, Mom did the laundry in the cellar. I hesitate to call it a basement, since the modern understanding of that term doesn't describe our cellar accurately. It was a brick-walled room under the kitchen accessible only from an outside door – more like a fruit cellar or a tornado refuge. The house above sat on brick pillars in a crawl space visible from the cellar. The house was uninsulated. One light bulb hung in the middle of the cellar, which was about 12 feet square, controlled by a string switch. Walking down the cellar stairs, entering the cellar, and picking your way through the dark to that string was always a scary experience. I always expected Frankenstein to jump out at me in the dark. That feeling of impending doom takes years to shake off.

One interesting food item was margarine, instead of butter which was very expensive – and unavailable during World War II. Thanks to the dairy industry lobby, an Iowa law prohibited margarine from being yellow, apparently to prevent folks from confusing it for butter. So it came as a white substance in a plastic container, with a tablet of yellow dye inside. To color the margarine, we had to break the tablet, and massage the bag to distribute the color evenly. Before long, it looked like butter. Many years later, some studies indicated that oleomargarine was not beneficial to arterial health, but we sure enjoyed it spread thickly on a fresh, steaming slice of homemade bread. Those who were children in the 1940s remember the triumph of margarine. It was often their job, after all, to turn the white, lard-like stuff into something resembling edible.

Dad had a privilege that made me look forward to being the head of the house one day. He had the luxury of having two pork chops or two burgers at supper, which was twice the number that we kids got. We backfilled the shortfall with extra potatoes or a peanut butter sandwich later if necessary. Mom had what I would call an "open" kitchen. I guess she didn't think of her role as including waiting on everybody, so she permitted full and unrestricted access to whatever the kitchen had to offer, so long as we tidied up afterward. We often had to do the dishwashing as well, and I still bear an inch-long scar on my left wrist acquired while washing dishes and testing a cracked water glass by squeezing it at the open end. Four stitches at Dr. Wiedemeyer's office convinced me that such experiments weren't in my best interest.

Mom's washing machine was one of those electric open top models with a water basin for excruciatingly hot water and soap, and a pair of wringers on the rim to squeeze the water out of the clothes. In 8th grade shop class, I worked hard to make Mom a laundry stick, which looked like a three foot long two-pronged wooden fork, so she wouldn't have to stick her hands in that hot water to lift the clothes out. The following year she got one of those new Maytag automatic washers making her need for the stick obsolete. She kept that stick around though for years – mainly as a deterrent for two mischievous young boys.

Some of the mischief was amazingly creative. When Mick was about two or three years old, Mom wanted him to play outside on the north side of our home on Tyler Street, but he was prone to wander off. So she tied a rope to his overalls (very common little boy wear in those days) and the other end to the clothesline. He was able to move back and forth along the clothesline, and from side to side about 20 feet or so.

After a while, Mom looked out and saw that Mick had disappeared. His overalls were still tied to the clothesline, but they were just a crumpled pile on the ground with no Mick. He was not wearing a shirt, and he had no underwear on, which caused Mom to panic, yelling at me to get outside and look for him. I had no luck finding him for several minutes, but then Mom called me back to the house. Mick had been found. Mr. Wilkins, owner of the Rexall Drug Store on the corner of Tyler Street and Floyd Avenue had just called and said Mick was outside drinking from the always-flowing water fountain located on the corner and naked as the day he was born.

Mom told me to watch baby Lynda, while she ran the nearly three blocks down to Wilkins Drug to retrieve him. Remember the earlier description of the always flowing water fountain? Mom learned when she got to him that he had been drinking from the overflow dog bowl at ground level because he was too short to reach the bubbler. By the time he got home the only feature I noticed was the red bottom he had apparently acquired on the way back home.

I hesitate to relate the next story of Mick's and my young misadventures, but the consequences of our behavior did have a positive ending. In 1948, I had seen the movie about Joan of Arc, starring Ingrid Bergman as the French religious icon and war heroine who was burned at the stake. In my 10 year-old judgment, I thought that was astonishing and I thought it would be wonderful to replicate the activity. So —— Mick and I decided to tie our sister Lynda to a tree, build a fire under her, and —— well, you know the rest.

Of course we never carried our plot out, since just the tree-tying nearly sent my Mom into orbit. It was the first time she ever whipped me, but in an unusual way. I had to go "cut my own switch" off one of the many trees in our vicinity, bring it back to her and she would administer the punishment accordingly. Imagine! The mental torment before the whacking was excruciating! I just couldn't pick out a switch that was going to be painless.

Health wasn't a serious concern in our home, since most of the time we had very healthy lives. We had the childhood diseases naturally, one by one. Living so intimately to the outdoors also apparently exposed us to all of the allergens, which luckily helped me develop an allergy-free life, confirmed by the allergist with the needle tests. No hay fever, no sniffles, no rashes, no problem. I consider it a blessing, but I don't know how I had such good fortune.

However, around 1948, the polio epidemic struck Leeds and pandemonium shot across the town like a flash. Hastily, many people pulled in and isolated themselves. Our Roberts Dairy milkman, a man named Reno, regrettably contracted the disease and died shortly thereafter. That injected abject fear into everyone in Leeds. Nobody knew how it was contracted, much less what it was. Only four years later, in 1952, Jonas Salk came up with a polio vaccine, and the disease today is hardly ever known.

VII.

Values: Caught more than taught

"Life isn't about finding yourself. Life is about creating yourself."
— George Bernard Shaw

It's difficult to reflect on one's early life without considering the impact of parents and Grandparents. After many years, I realized that many of my experiences with my parents may have been strongly influenced by my parents' own experiences in their youth. Mom was such an excellent student in school that she skipped fourth grade. She was a voracious reader, and graduated from Central High School in Sioux City with honors. She was highly literate, and knowledgeable about many things. Her greatest enjoyment and skill was playing word games (Scrabble, Boggle, crossword puzzles, etc.), and she was indomitable at them.

My Dad, in contrast, quit school after the eighth grade, enlisted in the Civilian Conservation Corps and participated in public works construction while still a teenager. He was highly self-controlled, but not interested in being a reader in those years. No question that he was a high energy, high production dynamo when it came to work or doing physically demanding things. He remodeled our dining room our first year in the Central Avenue house, including converting all the passageways to open archways without doors, save for bedrooms and the bathroom. In the second year, he remodeled the kitchen, building all new cabinets, counter top, and a breakfast nook that we actually used for the evening meal for the whole family. Like many carpenters' homes, our house was never finished. He built a new garage, added a closed-in back porch, converted the coal shed to a screened in sunroom, remodeled my sister's bedroom, adding built in cabinets and drawers.

His work ethic was a model for me that set a very high standard.

However, the relationship with each of my parents produces diverse memories – some good, some less so.

Most positive feelings that stay with me about my childhood emanate largely from my warm and pleasant memories of the love and esteem I received from my Mother. I never doubted that she loved me, and her praise and regard about my accomplishments comprise some of my fondest recollections. She had immense faith that I would benefit from advanced schooling and encouraged my commitment to scholarship. One of the most pleasant memories is of when I would come home from school, and she would sit down with me and discuss my day and experiences. She exuded sincere interest and thoughtfulness in whatever I was doing– highly valued by any child.

While she was warm and loving, she could occasionally have a pinch of irritability. For example, I'll admit that sometimes I was more than a little disrespectful and argumentative with her – typically a teenager's disposition. Faster than a speeding bullet, she would give me a slap up the right side of my head before I could react. Because she was left-handed, I never saw it coming. I will say I never got a smack that I thought I didn't deserve, and her infrequent eye-opening, physical rebukes made sure I was heading in the right direction as a person. Mom's chastisements were always delivered with "hard love."

Mom's mother, Kate, was my beloved Irish Grandmother. She was 100% Irish, born of Irish immigrants in 1898, married a navy veteran, John L Schultz, in 1915, bore 7 children, the third of which was my mother. My Grandfather Schultz died suddenly while working on the job at the Woodbury County Courthouse due to a sudden heart attack in 1940 when he was only 54. Gram, as we called her, remained a widow and single parent the rest of her life. She lived in Crescent Park on

28th Street just west of George Street in Sioux City. Gram was always a presence in our lives since we saw her frequently, usually for Sunday dinner at least. She was a highly resourceful woman, with sewing skills that enabled her to stay employed as an alterations seamstress during even hard times up until she retired.

John Leo Schultz About 1910   *Cathryn Irene Flanagan Schultz – About 1912*

Grandpa John (people called him Jack) was a distinguished man in our family history. His service in the U.S. Navy was as a Fireman 1st Class while on the steamship Michigan in the Atlantic from 1908 to 1912. He later became the operating engineer in the Woodbury County Courthouse, which to this day remains a historical landmark.[53] At one time, it was the tallest building for hundreds of miles around, and one of the renowned public landmarks of the Great Plains with its "Prairie School" architecture, akin to the style made famous by Frank Lloyd Wright.

---

[53] Donald Kaul, in his *Des Moines Register* column once called the Woodbury County Courthouse "the best building in Iowa – period." The building, designed by architect William Steele, was listed on the National Register of Historic Places in 1996.

Sioux City, Built 1918, Arch- W. L. Steele

Woodbury County Courthouse 1918

Early in their marriage, Kate and John lived in the courthouse, until their 4th child (John) came along. Mom (born 1919 – the 3rd child) used to share stories of how she and her older sister, Clarice, would run the elevator up and down from the basement to the roof when the courthouse was closed on the weekends.

I was only about 18 months old when my Grandfather Schultz died, but Mom told many stories about him and his gentle nature. Once, when both my grandfathers were at our home visiting, I was crawling on the living room floor. Both Grandpa John and Grandpa Neil bent down and called for me to come to them simultaneously. What might have embarrassed them was thwarted when according to Mom, I looked at one, then at the other, and then sat up and began to cry without showing any favoritism to either of them. Mom said that was definitely proof that I would someday be a mediator peacemaker – she said that my response was absolutely flawless given the circumstances.

I always felt blessed because of the colorful and fascinating perspectives of Gram Schultz. Widowed, and 100% Irish,, she was fond to take time to tell me stories about family and activities that were enchanting. She was never well off financially, but she was one of the most generous people I ever knew. She was a romantic, telling us of her Flanagan brothers (Tom, Pat, and Mike) who had been Vaudeville performers, singers and dancers. They and many other Irish relatives were the protagonists of many of her stories. Gram also came from a very large family, which meant lots of weddings and funerals.

Cathryn Irene (Flanagan) Schultz 1975

One of my favorite memories is of going to Gram's Mother's (my Great Grandmother's) house in the "South Bottoms" on Steuben Street near the confluence of the Floyd and Missouri Rivers. We called her "little Grandma," but she was my Great-Grandmother Mary Ann Byrne Flanagan, who came from Ireland in 1885. We went to her home once for a wake being held for one of the Gram's elderly brothers who had passed away. Since it was called a "wake," I wasn't sure what the expectations were, but I hoped it didn't mean that my great-uncle would wake up. The setting was straight out of an Irish novel, with my great-uncle laid out in a casket in the living room with a priest in attendance, where the descriptor "somber" was an understatement. In the dining room, a huge repast was laid out, with several women preparing and serving mounds of delicious looking and smelling food. The male contingent was in the kitchen, where they were drinking toasts to the dearly departed with an appropriate Irish whiskey.

A picture of that event, my first funeral, is burned into my memory, as is the admonition from Gram to "not go upstairs" in Little Grandma's house, because she "keeps a tiger up there." I found out years later my fears were misplaced because it wasn't a tiger, but simply where Uncle Happy [his nickname – he was actually Francis or Frank] had his bedroom. I don't know how he got the nickname of "Happy," but I do remember him as a gentle, friendly guy. Gram Schultz' family was the most frequent source of social gatherings and conviviality over the years – leaving me filled with endless memories.

As everyone knows, growing up is a mix of enjoyable times and not so enjoyable times. Some of my experiences as a youth – particularly disciplinary experiences – occasionally were disagreeable. Some things might even have gotten close to abusive by contemporary definition. What I mean by that is my Dad was extremely intolerant of misbehavior, especially dialogue that he referred to as back talk (he called it "contradicting him." – I think that was the biggest word in his vocabulary and he liked invoking it). He had little flexibility or tolerance when one of his rules was violated. He was the <u>Dad</u> and that trumped any possible argument you might offer.

I loved my Dad and certainly respected him, but sometimes I feared the ground he walked on. Most of my own miscreant acts I think were mostly typical of boys. But, occasionally my Dad seemed reluctant to be lenient or compassionate toward his sons, while extremely tolerant and enabling for his daughter. I don't remember him ever spanking Lynda – I think he was convinced that females had more delicate or fragile physicality that could be harmed. However, Dad demanded obedience from me and Mick without a speck of slack.

Dad's discipline was harsh, swift, and certain – when he had knowledge of some of my transgressions. What a blessing it is that he didn't know of all of them. Like the time Bob Harward, Dick Watt, and I decided to manufacture hard (alcoholic) cider. We bought a gallon of apple cider drank a little bit of it, threw in some raisins and yeast, and let it sit for a long time – about half an hour. We then drank it, and promptly got sick and tossed our cookies.

Or the time when we all were out on Halloween trick or treating for candy when we decided to tip over one of the many outhouses in town that were still in use. We came upon an outhouse (sometimes called a "tassy") in someone's back yard, all got on it and started to rock the wooden phone-booth size building, when some man inside yelled in a menacing voice, "WHAT'S GOING ON OUT THERE?" We stopped immediately and took off. I don't know what Dad would have done if he knew of such things. I was blessed not to find out.

Mick and I occasionally received whippings with my Dad's belt, and the strokes would leave heavy, purplish-black belt-shaped bruises on our upper legs and backsides.

Not surprisingly, these marks were very embarrassing to us when dressing for physical education classes in the boys' locker room at Leeds High School. Those occasional beatings persisted until I was fourteen years of age, when finally I stood and took the punishment in silence without flinching. He never whipped me with a belt again, but he did try to clobber me with his fist a few times when I talked back like most teenage boys do occasionally. I learned to duck and dive for the door when he was in a fury.

Mom (Wilma) and Dad (Ken) – at 25th Anniversary, 1963

In a way, he was reserved with compliments, but when they came – even though they were few and far between – those comments were truly precious. Sometimes I had a feeling that the absence of criticism from Dad was actually unspoken praise.

No one reaches adulthood without heaps of support from friends, teachers, and most importantly, family. Both parents gave me support, even on those occasions when I couldn't always rely on other people or friends. Definitely the single biggest attribute I acquired within my family, was from my mother — she exemplified a sensitivity and concern for others. Her example of caring for others taught me more than anything she said.

I read once why some people, referred to as "rescuers," in World War II Germany and other European countries chose to hide Jews from the Nazi extermination machine at risk of their own lives. The research studies about the causes and what prompted such high-risk actions lay in the nature of the rescuer's upbringing. A sensitive, caring parent who lived a model of altruism and selflessness did more to produce children that would respond when other human beings were in need or in danger, with little or no thought for themselves. On the other hand, stern and strict authoritarian parents imparted opposite sensitivities. For the rigid, autocratic parent, the concern of going about one's business and task orientation was greater than a concern for people.

An example was once when I was about 14, I was working (driving nails) with Dad on a house he and Gramps were building. I had learned the nomenclature of the parts of a claw hammer from Levi Deedrick, my industrial arts teacher. So while working, driving nails, I paused and said to Dad, "You know Dad – this hammer (in my hand) has many parts and I know some of them. I pointed at a couple of points, and said, "This is the face, and the top of the claw here is the ogive." He quickly spat out a rejoinder, "Don't give me that crap – get back to driving nails." There was little or no romance in work for Dad.

So, ironically, I believe I had parents of both types. Mom was caring and sensitive, encouraging me at every turn. Dad was judgmental, setting the bar high to please him, and very assertive in disciplinary actions. No one in the family dared challenge Dad's authority. If he said "don't contradict me" once, he said it a thousand times. However, it didn't crush my soul as it perhaps does to some, but I developed my own compliant and accommodating self. I just dealt with it.

I'm confident that I benefitted from both those parental characteristics and traits. I know that I care a great deal about people, even teaching Bible classes on Christian grace and justice to adult classes in

95

church, about how important it is to help provide justice to the poor and vulnerable. But I also know that I am highly goal oriented, perfectionist in my work, and I strive unrelentingly hard for accomplishment. I was used to working to please Dad, and it metamorphosed into working to please myself with a job well done.

Oddly, my Dad never said, "I love you," to me, nor to any of my siblings that I know of, any time while growing up. In fact, it took six decades after I had thoroughly demonstrated success in life before Dad told me he loved me and then it seemed fleeting and very subdued. I never understood why, but a few years after that when I had to loan him $25,000 temporarily so he could make a down payment on a new home while waiting for his former home to sell, he said to me in a quiet voice, "you were always the good child." I was perplexed and wondered if that was as close to an apology for his occasionally authoritarian nature. I'll never know, but I hold no animosity toward his inexplicable behavior. I've forgiven him his transgressions toward me, and it's one of those things that compel me to tell my kids and grandkids frequently that I love them. I guess it's called "the blessing." Some people get it from their parents, but I never did from Dad until very late in life. At least I got it however late it came.

Paradoxically, Dad's parents – my Grandparents, Neil and Ethel Poston – were very positive and engaging people in my life. I remember once when Gramps (as we affectionately called him) was visiting our house doing some business with Dad. He was preparing to drive back to his home, so I sneaked into the back seat floor in his car and stowed away for the drive to his home about three blocks away. When we reached his home, he discovered me and simply chuckled. I spent the rest of the afternoon watching him work in his basement woodshop where he had a ShopSmith system. No penalty for stowing away, except for the 15 minute walk home later.

Ethel (Gram) and Neil (Gramps) Poston in 1965

Gram Poston was always warm and welcoming, maybe because I was her first-born grandchild. In any case she was always the source for some warm cookies or other pastry from the oven. Sometimes when we had the whole family around, and she did expect proper decorum from grandchildren in her kitchen. I saw her shoo my cousin, Gary Clark, out of the kitchen, and he unexpectedly took a swing at her and caught her billowing dress. She swung around quick as a wink and gave him a slap that sounded like a popgun. Gary went down, and I'm sure he (and I) learned that Gram Poston wasn't one to antagonize – at least without consequences anyway.

One of Gram Poston's attributes was a passion for cleanliness and order – something I must have inherited from her, and I'm sure that it was inherited by my Dad. Gram's home was always immaculate, and extremely well kept, even when she moved into an unpretentious little old house on Van Buren Street after they lost their home after the Leeds flood of 1953. In all of her homes, I enjoyed the fresh and buoyant smell of Gram's sheets when I slept there a few times. It was like sleeping on a magic carpet for me.

I got to stay with Gram and Gramps Poston on the very rare occasions when my folks were traveling, and Gram's house helped me appreciate spotless home environments.

Gram and Gramps' (as we called them affectionately) youngest daughter, Karen – my Dad's younger sister and my aunt – was only two years older than I was, and attended the same schools, so she was really like my older sister. She was the Homecoming Queen at Leeds High school when I was a sophomore, and I couldn't have been prouder to be her nephew. I also valued her counsel – she once suggested that I get some white buck shoes, some charcoal gray slacks, and a white turtle-neck sweater. I listened, I got them, and I harvested some encouraging looks and attention from girls in the high school. At fifteen years of age, my "social persona" changed, making me feel upbeat about my appearance. Amazing what a few clothes can do for one's esteem.

Karen was also a member of the Leeds High School Girls' basketball team, which in those days was played six on six, with 3 girls from each team assigned to the two half courts of the basketball floor. So, basically, the game was played on half of the court at a time with three girls on offense from one team and three girls on defense from the other team. Karen was tall, so she was a real standout among her peers.

Leeds High Girls Basketball Team 1953

Left to Right: Karen Poston, Jean Olsen, Carolyn Crouch, Karen Roeper, Donna Stewart, Charlotte Tozier, Connie Ives, and Bonnie Ives

Karen was always a very positive influence on my life, especially when she helped me obtain a scholarship for college after my senior year of high school. As I've said many times, she was like the best sister I could ever have had.

RELIGION BRINGS FOCUS AND DEPTH – ALBEIT GRADUALLY

The earliest recollection I have about religious activity had to do with a baby chicken. Early in life – I think I was about 5 or 6 years old – I received a "purple" baby chick from my Crescent Park first grade (Miss Rellen) teacher to commemorate Easter (in 1944). The little creature had been dyed the color of light purple, and my classmate's chickens had been died pink, blue, green, and other pastel colors. Well, predictably my chick died after a brief life of two days and I was heartbroken. Mom, who was always sympathetic, said the best thing to do was to have a funeral and to pray for the baby chicken.

So knowing little about the protocols of death, I made a little casket out of pasteboard and a cross out of two Popsicle sticks. I dug a grave in the vacant lot north of our house at the southwest corner of 28th and George Street, and buried the chicken. The funeral was rather unpretentious, but somehow it was comforting – foreshadowing my future relationships with Jesus and God. Without knowingly forgetting to do so, I failed to mark the grave. When I drove by that site last year, I noticed that there is now a house on that lot. I hope it isn't haunted by a little baby chick.

My spiritual development, like most people's, was conditioned by my home life. Mom was Irish and Catholic, and her moral perspectives were clear as a bell and reflected a highly conservative and extensive code of personal behavior centering on justice and moral righteousness. Mom had some aphorisms that she used when I might be feeling down that were always uplifting. Sometimes I just had to figure out what gifts I had to cope with whatever challenge I was facing.

Of course, Dad had a code of conduct too, but it wasn't highly related or even connected to a religion. Dad left school at the end of the eighth grade at Woodrow Wilson Junior High School in Sioux City, and entered the world of work. Dad avoided church experiences nearly all of the time for himself, although he wouldn't discourage me if I wanted to go to church, which I often did. However, Dad wanted nothing to do with the Catholic Church, including having me attend the local Catholic school, St. Michael's, in Leeds. I heard later that he had steered clear of Catholicism after he and a priest got into a shouting match over birth control shortly after he and Mom were married. Dad was not one to be pushed around, even where his salvation or religious beliefs were concerned.

Consequently, most of my interactions with the church were self-initiated. I was baptized twice: once as an infant[54] and again in 1946 at the Wesley Methodist Church in Leeds.

I learned that religion is more often "caught" than taught, and I caught a major lesson in Christian love when I started Sunday school at the Wesley Church. Since Dad didn't go to church, and Mom as I said earlier was Catholic, I was on my own. When I was about 7 years old or so, they sent me down the street (three blocks) to the Methodist church for my first Sunday school experience. I meandered a little bit, and I remember I was very reluctant to even go. Consequently, I was a little late. I finally found my way to the right class, and walked in. Everyone stopped what

---

[54] My first baptism was at St. Boniface Catholic Church in Sioux City as an infant when we lived at 200 Perry Street on the west side of downtown Sioux City, and the second time was three blocks south of our home at 4548 Central Avenue in Leeds when I was seven years old. The Methodist pastor was Reverend Joseph Castle.

they were doing, and looked at me. I nearly bolted back out the door, but "Toot" (Henrietta) Harward – the teacher and my best friend's Mom – jumped up and exclaimed, "Billy, we've been waiting for you! Come on in and join us." That one act of welcoming kindness did more to keep me interested in church stuff than anything. Her example was worth a life time of sermons, and much more persuasive.

I had my ups and downs with religion –I was the lone member of my family that attended church more or less regularly. Once I even delivered a speech at school on the topic of eternal life – as if I knew much about that. Nevertheless, it was well received. At least I don't remember getting heckled. See the article below.

The Leader

Volume 31   LEEDS HIGH SCHOOL, Sioux City, Iowa   April 6, 1955

Janice Harward Wins State Post

Janice Harward, president of Leeds FHA chapter, was elected vice-president of the Iowa Association of Future Homemakers of America at the annual leadership conference held at the Hotel Savery in Des Moines last week.

Appearing in all three day's program, Janice took part in a panel discussion with seven other girls, demonstrated as part of the candidate's carnival how to make a terry cloth wrap, and the last morning was installed as vice-president.

Janice will as part of her duties of the vice-presidency be expected to plan and preside at a northwest district meeting.

From July 18-22 she will attend the national FHA convention to be held at Ames. She will meet two days each in August and January with other officers and their advisors to help plan the district and state leadership conferences.

"Eternal Life" Is Thursday's Topic

"Eternal Life" will be the theme for tomorrow's Holy Week services at Wesley Methodist church at 8 o'clock. Speakers on this subject will be Ida Shoop and Bill Poston.

The YMCA and YWCA with the help of city ministers are sponsoring the city-wide program of Holy Week services. Leeds co-chairmen are Tom Porsch and Connie Clawson.

"Count Your Christian Blessings' has been the theme used for the services this year. Sharon Hooks and Tom Hooker spoke on Freedom Monday. The subject of Faith was discussed by Lois Shively and Allan Rarick on Tuesday and this morning Charlotte Johnson and Roger Oosten gave talks on Hope.

Many Students Help With Service

Others who participated in this week's program were Frances Sisson, F. E. Davis, Jo Ann

(Con't. on Page 4)

Leeds to Hold 1955 Pa Sponsored by the Stude

Thirty-two thousand pounds of newspapers and 15,000 pounds of magazines collected last year in

Paper Drive Ends With Sock Hop

If you've succeeded in getting your socks clean since the March 4 sock hop, you'll be happy to hear you can wear them again a week from Friday night at the dance which will conclude the paper drive.

On April 15 the student council will sponsor the dance which will begin at 8 o'clock and end at 11:30. A king and queen with attendants will be a feature of the dance, with the royalty chosen by homerooms with the most sen by homerooms with the most

Judy Hamilton and Beverly Carlson were appointed as co-chairmen for the dance. Margaret Calhoun is in charge of publicity;

Leeds
the m
be he
dent
Apr
to ele
winter
Since
day th
days,
conclu
and se

Hon
most
queen,
dance.
be all
queen,
ner.
Pap
Pap
111 T
studer
The

Leader article about eternal life speech April, 1955

Note in the *Leader* above, that Janice Harward also was featured for winning the Future Homemakers of America chapter vice presidency, earning her an all expenses trip to Des Moines, our state capital. Also, of lesser significance was an article about an upcoming "Sock Hop," which was a dance where shoes had to be left at the door. The co-chair of that event was Judy (Hamilton) Moore – my "steady" at the time. You can see why all of us felt special with individual recognition – thanks to our small school size.

Back to the focus on my eternal soul — it's funny how some memories come back to us when we reflect on going to church. I remember that the church gave me a Bible when I moved from 6th grade to 7th grade in September 1951. It even had my name in it. I carried it back and forth, walking down the Central Avenue hill to church and back up the street to my home every week. I felt very protective of that Bible, but once on a rainy day, I jumped the flowing rain water along the curb and dropped that precious book (to me at least) in about 4 inches of running muddy water. I was devastated, and I remember crying all the way home. Mom comforted me, took it under her wing, wiped it off, and laid it out to dry in the kitchen. Despite some wrinkled pages, it still served me well until I lost it in a devastating fire in 1983.

Other than Easter and Christmas, religious activities in our home were very limited. I was very surprised when Reverend Castle asked my Grandpa Poston to make an attractive baptismal font out of oak with an oak cross as the handle on the lid. Gramps did a beautiful job (he was a tremendous woodworker and carpenter) and I felt like I "owned" part of that church because that font was made by <u>my</u> Gramps!

Incidentally, we (or at least I did) attended the Methodist Church in Leeds some years after my Dad had a falling out with the Catholic priest over family planning (birth control). That squabble may persist today in many homes.

Of course, with Mom coming from a big Irish Catholic family, the Flanagans were constantly having wedding masses, funerals, and occasions when attending mass was important. Mom had what seemed like a dozen aunts and uncles – all Irish, all Flanagans, and some that died from time to time. The funerals were a remarkable combination of grieving and celebrating the deceased's life. I always enjoyed the Irish "wakes," which combined of a viewing of the deceased in the front room of their home, and a celebration of his or her life. Irish funerals were seldom sad affairs – they were more like celebrations. It was fun to say the least.

It is said that personal values are more often "caught" than "taught." In my case, that was certainly true when it came to spiritual matters of the heart. My mother used to quote something close to Philippians 2:3 when she would address my feelings of self-aggrandizement from time to time by declaring to me, "You are no better than anyone else, but you're just as good." Her homilies were few and far between, but when they came, they were perfectly on target.

I was fortunate to win the American Legion Citizenship Award twice – once at graduation, and four years before at the end of 8th grade. I received a medal at my graduation in 1957 in front of my family, friends, and neighbors. I felt humbled since the honor was bestowed by vote of the faculty.

However, when I previously earned a similar Citizenship award at the end of the 8th grade in 1953, it was presented by a confused American Legionnaire. The Legionnaire announced, "The winner of the Distinguished American Legion Citizenship Award is" (and then he squinted at the certificate) and read, "Miss <u>Lillian</u> Poston." The auditorium erupted in raucous laughter for what I felt was an eternity. When I walked up to receive the award, the Legionnaire didn't seem to notice I was not a Lillian. I'm sure he might have been a veteran of the Spanish-American War in 1898 or even earlier.

Speaking of names, mine was actually "Billy" from the time I was born until I reached high school, when I dropped the 'y.' In spite of this, my two grandmothers – Ethyl Taylor Poston and Cathryn Irene Schultz – never stopped calling me Billy. I was also a 'Jr' since my name was the same as my Dad's. Mom told one of my daughters that Dad's parents had always called him Ken or Kenny. When Gram Poston was asked why he was named William but called Ken, she simply replied, "We liked Ken." I don't know what that means for my name – second best I guess.

With the same name as Dad, I never had the experience of receiving any mail addressed to me that hadn't been opened. My Dad's explanation was that he thought my mail was addressed to him, since it had his name on it. I am sure that he didn't think that the magic coder ring I ordered from the *Sky King* Radio show[55] was for him, but he always opened all my mail anyway. That problem didn't resolve itself, until I left home shortly after graduating from high school at Dad's suggestion.

I also was fortunate in 1954 to win first prize in the local Chamber of Commerce essay contest. My "I speak for Democracy" essay was the regional winner, and I received a complete set of the encyclopedia, *Book of Knowledge.*

Grolier's Book of Knowledge Encyclopedia – First Prize

That was a great resource for several years afterward. I still remember standing up in front of the whole student body and delivering my essay in

---

[55] The *Sky King* Radio Show featured many neat items, decoder rings, Morse code rings, etc. The sponsor was Peter Pan Peanut Butter, and I saved the labels from the jars and sent them in with some gratuitous fee, usually 25¢ or so.

person. It was humbling, to say the least, but I felt good about being fortunate enough to be selected for the distinguished honor. Like many things later in life, the tangible rewards that were fascinating and appreciated were not as noteworthy as was the esteem of my friends and colleagues.

Learning about people from other races and nationalities was difficult in Leeds. Leeds was pretty lily-white back in the day. No African-Americans lived in Leeds then, nor were there any Hispanic families. I wish there had been. There were some Native American families in the area, and my Dad and Grandad frequently employed them in their construction business. At age 14, I worked with a number of Native American workers from the Winnebago Sioux Reservation in a summer job with Dad, and I found them to be very congenial and fun to work with as I learned some of the craft of construction.

Bill Poston Wins Speech Contest

Bill Poston, Sr. 12, will represent Leeds high school in the Voice of Democracy contest sponsored by the Sioux City Junior Chamber of Commerce.

Bill was selected from four other contestants—Dick Ludwig, Dick Landers, Kay Koontz, and Tom Hooker—in the project in which the entire speech class, under the direction of Mrs. Mary Ellen Frakes, took part. High school teachers acted as judges for the school contest.

All participants prepared a 5-minute broadcast script on the subject, "I Speak for Democracy" which were delivered orally in competition with other students. The five speakers from whose essay Bill's was chosen, were selected by the speech class.

On November 16, Bill transcribed his speech at KTRI, along with the winners from other Sioux City high schools. These recordings will be used to select community semi-finalists.

Winning the "I Speak for Democracy" Contest, 1956

My first close up and personal experience with African-Americans was when we played Boys' Town in Pop Warner football in Omaha. I must have been 11 or 12 years old and played on the Roberts Dairy team. I remember I weighed 117 pounds, but the limit was only 112 pounds. Bill Lyle, the coach (and a Leeds High alumnus), waived my 5 pounds so I could participate on the team. Bill was one of my favorite adults – a real pure heart.

We once took a bus to Omaha (100 miles south), and played the Boys' Town team on their indoor field. Boys Town was a Catholic boarding school for orphaned boys of all races and classes. It was a challenging football game for us, and the hardest part was keeping up with the seasoned orphaned kids. But the fun part was skinny dipping in the school's indoor pool after the game. I became well acquainted with ethnic differences from the gaggle of boys from both teams in the swimming pool, and I learned that such things really didn't matter. That first close contact with kids of very different races turned out to be a very positive encounter. It's hard to be officious or jaundiced by any kind of ethnic arrogance when everyone, including you, is stark naked and having harmless fun.

Our team was sponsored by Roberts Dairy in Sioux City, and our team practiced on a field adjacent to the dairy. After practice we were invited to visit the dairy to watch the milk production lines, and we were mesmerized by the manufacture of cottage cheese in huge rectangular stainless steel vats in which the worker, in sterile hip boots, waded around and stirred up the mixture. It was a good example of how some things are more appealing if you don't know how they're made. Occasionally, the workers would give us a free quart of milk in a plasticized cardboard container. I loved it. While in the State of Iowa, Roberts Dairy was my dairy. Late in life, after a 28-year absence out of Iowa, I returned and picked up where I left off with Roberts Dairy, even though our home was 200 miles away from Sioux City. Several years later, I was more than a little disappointed to see that Roberts Dairy was taken over by a larger company – Hiland Dairies. Roberts is no more, but my memories about that exciting dairy are as vivid today as they were 65 years ago.

Still another experience which remains prominent in my memory was the honor of being elected a Homecoming attendant in the fall of 1956. Carol Farris, a girl in the June 1957 class had lost an arm due to a terrible accident early in life. The boys were asked who would "be willing" to accompany her in the procession and on the stage for the homecoming festivities. I volunteered. I never thought of Carol as any less than any of the rest of us. She was a very sweet person. The entire homecoming court was a great bunch of young men and women.

1956 Homecoming Court
On the left Al Hatler and Judy Jenkins (King and Queen). In the center from top down are Norma (Stewart) Merchant and Tom Galbreath, Rosemary (Larson) Sutton and Don Johnson, Jackie (Putman) Lahrs and Tom Hooker, and Dick Johnson and Lilas (Blumer) Hubert. On the bottom, far right are Joe Conley and Carolyn (Betsworth) Kawalke, and Carol Farris and I are in the center of the bottom row.

My Mom commented later on how proud she was of me to accompany Carol. Actually, I would have done it without a second thought. I owe to my Mother the conviction that all peoples, no matter how different, are of equal worth. She emphatically taught that no one person or group is better than any other in the eyes of God.

My childhood experiences with the Christian faith were often few and far between, but something always tugged at me to align myself on the side of faith in the Gospel of Jesus. I sang in the church choir, actively participated in MYF (Methodist Youth Fellowship), accepted Christ as personal Savior at age 14, and listened reverently to Reverend Joe Castle. Of course, I was also interested in impressing his daughter, Vicky, who was my "special interest" until they moved away before we entered seventh grade at Leeds High School. Even to this day, my early commitment to the Christian Gospel persists, strengthened a great deal more by heavy involvement in my faith and my family. Those early lessons have somehow penetrated my inner guidance system and keep me pointed in the right direction.[56]

DUTY, HONOR, COUNTRY

The Poston family has a very long and gallant history of service to the United States of America, extending to even before the Revolutionary War. Two of my Great-Great-Great-Great Grandfathers, Solomon Poston Sr., and William Patton, both served under General Washington during the war of rebellion against the British rule of George III.[57] Also, Solomon Poston Jr. served in the War of 1812 under General Jackson.

The Civil War (according to my Union ancestors) or the War Between the States (according to my Confederate ancestors) was served by a number of family members, with one of my Great-Great Grandfathers serving for the Union (Cornelius Hammond Russell) and another of my Great-Great-Grandfathers serving for the Confederacy (Fielden L.

---

[56] "I believe in Christianity as I believe that the sun has risen: not only because I see it, but because by it I see everything else." — C.S. Lewis

[57] The Revolutionary War was fought against the rule George III, King of England and separately of Ireland. Later, the two countries united and George became king of Great Britain, which included England, Wales, Scotland, and Ireland. Most of my ancestry had origins from those countries.

Poston, who died in the Elmyra, New York Prisoner of War Camp). My maternal Grandfather, John Leo Schultz, served in the U.S. Navy closely after the end of the Spanish-American War, and my Dad served in the USMC during World War II (see earlier discussion). Ironically, my Dad never talked about the war. Neither did the Civil War veterans, according to what I have read. The theory is that the sights and sounds of war are so terrifying and horrific that it's too painful to dwell on them and better to compartmentalize them in the back of your mind and try to forget about it.

Drum & Bugle Corps Marching on 4th Street in Sioux City 1952

Dad was an active member of the American Legion and I, my brother Mick, and my friend Bob Harward all participated in the American Legion Drum and Bugle Corps (see picture above). We competed numerous times with other Legion Drum and Bugle Corps, and we marched in the 4th of July parade in Des Moines, Iowa's capital city in 1951.

In Sioux City, the Drum and Bugle Corps met and practiced on the parking lot across from the Monahan Legion Club, and after practice, the boys were treated to a free Coke and a chance to explore the Legion Hall. In the third floor attic, we found a casket that piqued our curiosity.

We opened it, and to our horror, we saw the dead body of Adolph Hitler! We ran down the stairs screaming. Later we learned that it was just a mannequin dressed up with a mustache and costume resembling Adolf Hitler. The stage prop had apparently been used in some clandestine, but macabre, celebrations of the end of World War II.

I was always proud of my Dad's service in the war, and my love of country grew even more in high school, culminating in winning the Voice of Democracy contest for the Siouxland area in 1956. The prize was a certificate and ceremonial key, which were regrettably lost in our 1983 fire. Nevertheless, the feelings of pride in the American way of life have persisted.

My own military service, served in a time of relative peace and the Cold War, began ten days after my 17th birthday, when I enlisted in the National Guard in Sioux City. After high school, I transferred to the United States Marine Corps Reserve, serving until my military obligation of six years was completed in the fall of 1961. Three years later, I re-joined the National Guard, accepted a commission, served for eight more years commanding an artillery battery with 105 men, attaining the rank of Captain. The service may have gone longer, but when I became a Superintendent of Schools in Tucson, Arizona in 1974, it was no longer possible for me to give the time required to continue. However, I have never regretted having the opportunity to serve my country. And, we did win the Cold War.

VIII.

Schooling: Lessons from in and outside the classroom

"Instruction does much, but encouragement everything."
— Johann Wolfgang von Goethe

Life is a journey, in which we gather and store experiences in a cerebral "catalog" if you will, that guide and direct us through our years on this planet. Leeds offered such a wide number of life experiences for kids, and I have always valued the enormous impact of Leeds' lessons learned over the years. It was a phenomenal place to grow up.

We weren't wealthy, but I never experienced hunger, precipitated by missing a meal. It wasn't until later on that I realized food had to be either grown or purchased with funds earned. Economic perspective was slowly gathered until I fully appreciated the connection between work and money, and money and living. In retrospect, when my Dad was making only $15 a week driving a truck, it seems almost an impossible situation for a young couple, but given the costs of the day, it was apparently enough to provide a sustainable living. They could provide for a home, food, clothing, a car and gasoline, and have enough left over to go to the Milwaukee Weiner House café in downtown Sioux City after an occasional movie which at many theaters was 16¢ or less for admission.

My education began in Leeds with Kindergarten, at Hawthorne Elementary School on the northwest corner of 43rd Street and Central Avenue in January, 1944. The Kindergarten room, taught by Miss Coffey, had a most unusual science-environmental feature – a goldfish pond built on the south wall of concrete, about 1 foot deep, 3 feet wide and 4 feet long, which had a full complement of fish. Hawthorne School was built in 1892, so during its centennial celebration in 1992, I visited the school. The goldfish pond was still there, but I'm pretty sure those were not the same fish. The school closed in 2010 after a longevity seldom seen with schools in modern times.

Hawthorne Elementary School, 1891-2010

Another lesson I learned was that January in northwest Iowa can be brutal in terms of weather. Asserting my independence early in Kindergarten by walking the two blocks from my house to the school, I encountered glare ice at the east entrance to the school. I slipped, slid, and fell a number of times, until somehow I made it to the door. Imagine my surprise when I found that ice had frozen the door shut, and all of my 5 year old strength wasn't sufficient to pull it open. I banged on the door, which was ½ story above the basement floor (we called it the garden level) and ½ story below the first floor. The upshot of that was that no one could see me.

But, to my rescue came one of the truly dedicated, but non-certificated, "teachers" – actually the custodian, Mr. Joe Farley. He opened the door and let me in from the cold. He welcomed me, and he was my hero for years afterward. He was a good model for all of us in that he never uttered a harsh word to anyone. I know I sure liked him, especially since he came to work before daylight to get the building warmed up for us.

My motivation for an education was mixed due to the fact that Mom was a high school graduate and Dad wasn't. In the depth of the Great Depression, Dad had dropped out of Woodrow Wilson Junior High School after completing the 8th grade so he could then enlist in the Civilian Conservation Corps.[58] His CCC service took him to Arkansas, Missouri, and Iowa. In fact, he operated a bulldozer when the CCCs helped build the Iowa State University golf course and Springbrook State Park (west of Des Moines), a 930 acre park built by the CCC in 1934-35. He acquired a lot of practical knowledge and with his mechanical aptitude; he became a successful mechanic, heavy equipment operator and carpenter. Regrettably, he wasn't much into reading or education, like Mom was. Many years later, when I was in graduate school working on my doctorate, he once said to me that "I was overeducated for my own good." He also asked me when I would stop going to school and get a real job. I got a big kick out of his teasing.

This was a common contrast between my parents. Mom was a compassionate mother and pro-education, but Dad was silent on the subject – other than to let me know that I had to behave myself in school. Mom always made sure we did our homework, and cleared a place on the dining room table for me to do my work. Papers were prepared on a green-tinted paper tablet of 100 pages or so, with a slick cover bound at the top of the page that had Palmer's Penmanship charac-

---

[58] The Civilian Conservation Corps (CCC) was created in 1933 by President Franklin D. Roosevelt to provide work for young men who could not find jobs because of the Great Depression. By putting these men to work on resource conservation projects across the United States, President Roosevelt intended the CCC to help solve two of the country's most serious problems, unemployment and resource degradation. In Iowa, the CCC built parks and preserves, planted trees, worked on drainage projects and assisted farmers in soil conservation efforts.

ters for us to emulate. Those tablets were distributed free to us at school and lasted a long time if one was careful and thrifty.

Poston and Harward Kids – Bob with a broken arm (c. 1947)

From Left to Right: Bill, Janice Harward, Bob Harward, Mick, and Lynda

Mom loved to discuss – sometimes argue – ideas and things, Dad didn't. In retrospect, I know he had opinions, but wasn't very tolerant of disagreement with his ideas. Mom was a progressive-thinking Democrat, Dad was a hard-nosed Republican[59]. Mom would show affection

---

[59] There was a definite benefit to grow up observing my parents' widely divergent views on many social and political issues. I'm sure it helped me be more conscientious in evaluating points of view without some prejudice influencing my thoughts

by touch and hugs, Dad was aloof and detached. I remember once when I was about nine or ten years old, I was walking down Central Avenue with Dad, heading to Gramps' house, and after about a block, I developed a "Charley horse," an unfocused cramp in the leg that made it difficult to walk. Dad was one of those "suck it up" guys, and instead of sympathizing, he told me to go back home. I did, and I remember that I was hurt, but not from the Charley horse.

Once I was kidding with Mom when I came home from school in about the 10th grade and announced to her that I was quitting school to join the Marines. I still remember her icy penetrating stare into my eyes, and her almost snarling response, "Over my dead body!" I could tell she meant it, so I wisely chose not to bring that topic up again.

When I completed three college degrees in later years, Mom was there for all of my graduations, and I could hear her shout as I walked across the stage, "That's my son!" You can't ask for more support than that from a parent.

Travel was a limited activity in our family. I didn't realize until after I was married that my Granddad Poston had never travelled more than 150 miles from Cherokee County, Iowa where he was born. My Granddad Schultz had served in the U.S. Navy after the Spanish-American war, and extensively travelled the Atlantic aboard a battle-ship. His home in 1910 according to the 1910 US Census was on board ship. Later of course, Dad traveled half way around the world as well during World War II, serving with the Marines.

We didn't travel much, so when we did, it was something memorable. Visiting family, going fishing, or participating in some organizational activity. We once drove all the way to Wichita, Kansas to visit my Dad's brother, Junior (Cornelius Hammond Russell Poston Jr.) and his family. That was an interesting trip, since we drove from Topeka to Wichita on the then new Kansas Turnpike. I had never seen anything like it. Another family trip was to Chicago to visit my Great Aunt Maude (Taylor), where we experienced our very first in what was to be a long line of pizzas. Such trips were a revelation of sorts. I saw my first mass transit train in Chicago, nicknamed the "El" because it was elevated above the traffic and pedestrians. Such things were spectacular to a kid like me from Leeds.

Poston Kids En Route to Wisconsin 1948

Left to right: Mom, me, Lynda, Rosada (cousin), Aunt Florence, and Mick

One trip, memorable only because of its discomfort and distance, was when Mom and we three kids traveled in July of 1948 (I was nine years old) with my Great Uncle Dutch (Doug) Poston, Great Aunt Florence, and their daughter, Rosada, who was Mick's age. All seven of us crowded into Uncle Dutch's 1942 Plymouth Coupe and traveled over 300 miles to Alma, Wisconsin. I shudder to remember how small that vehicle was, and to realize how much we were crammed into that car – three adults in the front seat, and four kids in the back seat. To say it was claustrophobic is a serious understatement. When we finally arrived in Alma and crossed the bridge over the Mississippi River to meet Aunt Clarice who would take us to her home in Mondovi, Wisconsin, we almost fell out of Uncle Dutch's pressure cooker with exhaustion. I've been claustrophobic ever since.

It's more enjoyable to remember two other trips where I traveled with peers. The first was a trip with the Pop Warner football team to Boys Town and the other was a trip to the Iowa State Capitol in Des Moines to compete in a Drum and Bugle Corps competition. The highlight of our trip to the State Capitol was that we marched in an American Legion parade in downtown Des Moines in 1951. At the time — I would have been 12½ years old — and we traveled with the Sioux City American Legion Drum and Bugle Corps, of which I, my brother Mick, and my best friend, Bob Harward, were members.

Brother Mick and Bob Harward
Sons of the American Legion Drum & Bugle Corps 1951

We traveled by bus (old Highway 141 all the way) to Des Moines for the American Legion convention in order to compete in the Junior Division of the Legion's Drum and Bugle Corps contest. We were housed in a dormitory at Grandview College, on old US Highway 69 (East 14th Street) in north Des Moines. We not only won our division, but were fortunate to have our photograph appear in the *Des Moines Register*, as we marched in the American Legion parade.

American Legion Parade highlighted in
the Des Moines Register, *August 8, 1951*

Another big treat on that trip was a chance to visit the famous (now long gone) Riverview Amusement Park. And to ride the roller coaster. For a 12-year-old boy, a trip to the Iowa State Capitol was an enormous eye opener. To see the gold-plated dome,[60] to march in front of huge crowds, and to experience a short stay in a dormitory room on a real college campus was more than educational – it was extremely exciting.

Most people can attest to the phenomenon that many lessons I learned were outside of school. Bob Harward and I partnered up with Dick Watt and the three of us became "joined at the hip." We didn't think of ourselves as a gang, but we had our own unique appellation for the three of us – The BDB's (Bob, Dick, Bill or Bill, Dick, Bob) we became, but once in a while to help Dick gain some imagined rank, we would call ourselves the KLB's (using the last letter of our first names). We thought we were so clever. I don't think there's an inch within a ten mile radius of Leeds that we didn't explore together.

Getting to know the opposite sex was easy – most kids in Leeds would come out after the evening meal, which was called "supper" in our town and talk, play games under the street lights like hide and seek or kick the can, or race on foot up and down the street. In spur of the moment foot races, it was exasperating that Judy (Hamilton) Moore could always beat me. Despite my occasional chagrin, we nevertheless learned to appreciate the simple fun to be had without gadgets, electronics, or cybernetic social "interaction" or networks.

As we reached our teens, we would congregate in Don and Larry Johnson's basement to listen to the latest tunes. I fondly remember the first time we heard Elvis Presley, when he debuted on local radio with "Blue Suede Shoes." Other melodies of note were "Earth Angel," "The Great Pretender," "Only You," and "Rock Around the Clock" with Bill

---

[60] The Iowa Capitol building dome is covered with roofing material made from 23 karat gold. Iowa's capitol is only one of ten domed capitols left standing and among these architectural gems, Iowa's capitol building supports the largest dome.

Haley and the Comets. At some point, we began dancing in Don and Larry Johnson's finished basement – sometimes jitterbugging and sometimes slow dancing. Seems like eons ago now, but I have vivid memories of the Johnson's basement get-togethers. The only restriction was that Don and Larry's mother, Norma, made us keep the basement well illuminated and the music within tolerable levels.

Some of our BDB activities included some improbable uses of our snow-covered streets. As mentioned before, we would wait at 44th and Central for the Sioux City Bus, which turned and headed south there. We would sneak around to the back, crouch down on our haunches, grab the bumper, and the bus would move forward, allowing us to "skate" on our feet over the hard packed snow. We could hitch a "ride" all the way down to 41st Street undetected before letting go. We sometimes did it with someone's car, but they would object if they saw us, and threaten us with telling our parents. That stopped us. Nothing worse than having to explain to Mom or Dad why I did such stupid things.

Learning about sex was a hoot. Mainly because we didn't learn anything other than from the neighborhood streets. In the sixth grade, Bill Owings opened my eyes by telling me that my male organ, which heretofore had been referred to as my "wienie," was properly called a "penis." I thought he said "peanuts" and was truly perplexed before someone set me straight. Like all early teen boys, I was curious about women's anatomy. Their physical topography was mysterious, but the mysteries of the opposite sex didn't transform to action since young men were very circumspect and respectful in those days. Nevertheless, like all boys, we loved to talk about such things when we were away from parents and other kids.

However, my mother's Catholic perspectives about sex were unspoken except for frequent tangential admonitions to "be a nice boy," "keep yourself properly clothed," "don't ask questions that I will not or cannot answer," etc. I never heard my mother refer to, describe, or mention any anatomical body parts, especially the procreative parts that are never to be seen. I'm pretty sure she was certain she'd be struck dead if she ever said anything about sex or procreation. Dad was more earthy but also unspecific. He'd say things like, "be sure you wash that thing down there," and "when you're old enough, I'll explain things to you," etc. Ironically, I must never have gotten old enough, because he never explained "things" to me. Frankly, it's a wonder that I ever figured out social norms and proper behaviors related to relationships with the opposite sex. That's what life in the 1950's was like – "we don't speak of such things" – so I had to acquire what I needed to know from peers who frankly were as clueless as I was.

By the time I got to the high school, I had learned a few "swear words" or cussing as it was commonly called. I had been exposed to three types of profanity by that time – (1) bodily effluent or parts (the 's' and 'p' words, etc.), (2) religious (God's name in vain, etc.), and (3) vulgate carnal (the 'f' bomb, etc.). Of course, these eye-openers were disclosed to me in absolute secrecy and used only when in a "safe" crowd of peers that we trusted with our "covert knowledge."[61]

Many years later I learned from some sociological research studies that using profanity in communication generally has a detrimental effect on the perceived credibility of the communicator. That convinced me to be circumspect in my verbal interactions with people in order to not diminish other's perceptions of me. Besides, I was sure that if I ever transgressed the strict moral code of my mother, she would hunt

---

[61] When I was in about the tenth grade, Dad and his old Navy Seabee buddy, Harry Spencer, were installing the ductwork for our new furnace (our first forced-air heating and ventilation system) under the house in the crawlspace there, I heard them cussing about the work they were performing, using some colorful language – which, up to that point I didn't realize that they knew some of the "secret" words. I wondered at the time how they had penetrated our secret society to learn some of our clandestine vocabulary. Gullibility was a hobgoblin of ignorance in my teens.

me down and give me one of her left-handed slaps on the cheek. Actually, it wasn't that serious, but I still curtailed any inclinations to misbehave on dates accordingly. Perhaps I just wasn't much of a risk taker in that regard – besides, girls in those days were more morally responsible and proper than any boys I knew, so we just didn't try to do anything unseemly. Even if we did try to do something inappropriate, girls I knew were unbending in their insistence on respectable behavior in any case.

It would be disingenuous to deny that my friends and I occasionally exhibited some mischief. One of our mischievous excursions that occurred in my teens was brought on by a curiosity we had heard about a movie with a famous actress appearing with no clothes. Motivated to check it out, a carload of us drove over 100 miles all the way to Omaha to see Brigitte Bardot in a French movie, titled, "And God Created Woman." We paid the exorbitant admission fee of 50 cents,[62] only to suffer through a mostly boring French film with subtitles to see Miss Bardot dart across the screen from left to right for about 1/10 of a second without her clothes. Our overly ambitious expectations were dashed, and the lengthy ride back up to Leeds further deflated our libidos.

In high school it was fashionable to "go steady" – a form of adolescent monogamous exclusivity – one boy, one girl. My steady most of the time was Judy (Hamilton) Moore – a truly sweet and smart girl with solid moral principles. My first big date with Judy – I think it was a prom or something of the sort – was to take her to dinner at the Green Gables on Pierce Street before the dance. Trying to be suave and debonair, I ordered the fried shrimp – something I had never eaten before but it was one of the least expensive entrees. They came

---

[62] Movies in Sioux City ordinarily ranged from 10 to 16 cents in those days, with popcorn only a dime and candy bars a nickel.

and I wasn't sure how to hold them, but I ate the whole plate of shrimp – tails and all. Crunchy to say the least, but at least Judy didn't deride me for my cluelessness. I was belatedly embarrassed when I learned it wasn't customary to eat the crustaceans' tails. They have the consistency of a human fingernail, which is digestible, but the tail is immune to digestive system enzymes. Who knew? I had a lot to learn about comestibles and libations.

There are remembrances and vignettes of school experience that rattle around my brain – serving as a lieutenant in the student safety patrol and dancing around the May pole at Hawthorne Elementary School, meeting one of my best friends, Alan Hatler, who came to us from Arkansas, (where he had been taught by one of his teachers that the pronunciation for Sioux City was "Sy-ox" City). That was a hoot.

I know I learned a lot in school – how to read (and what good things to read),[63] history, science, mathematics, social relationships, citizenship and patriotism, and how to enjoy music and sports. Patriotism was one of the favorite themes in high school when the whole student body would gather in the Leeds High School gymnasium/auditorium and have group singing. A dimly lighted projector would flash the song's lyrics on a screen up on the stage, and we would all sing patriotic songs – "Over hill, over dale...the Army goes marching along..," "Anchors aweigh ... anchors away," "Off we go into the wild blue yonder, flying high...," "From the halls of Montezuma to the shores of Tripoli...," "Mine eyes have seen the glory of the coming of the Lord....," and

---

[63] The Leeds High School and the Leeds Public Library were treasure troves for me. We had study halls in the library those days, and I was fond of exploring many diverse types of literature. Alice Dawson, our school "Dean" and Latin teacher supervised the study hall, and once observed me reading *Idylls of the King* by Tennyson, and asked if I was enjoying it. Frankly, I'm not fond of poetry, but I was interested in the Arthurian legends, so I answered "yes" and persevered all the way through it. It probably did me some good, but I still am not fond of poetry but enjoy ancient English history.

many others. It was fun and moving – I think it gave all of us a sense of belonging to something bigger than ourselves and maybe helped glue the disparate complexities of our free society together.

I also learned the consequences of irresponsible behavior. In sixth grade, while operating the safety stop sign on the northeast corner of 44th Street and Harrison Street, I filled some "down time" by playing with my Duncan yo-yo. Mabel Landon, my teacher, could see me from her room on the top floor, and relieved me of my rank of lieutenant for dereliction of duty. I felt very embarrassed to no longer have any safety patrol authority. Lesson learned.

We also learned the Pledge of Allegiance in school – twice. First we learned it as Francis Bellamy wrote it without the words, "under God" in it. We learned it again in 1955 when those words were added by the U.S. Congress. The pledge was originally accompanied with a salute facing the flag with the right arm raised up and extended toward the flag – commonly known as the "Roman Salute." But when Nazi Germany adopted the same salute, the U.S. Congress changed the American Flag salute to a simple, but very solemn, right hand over the heart. I don't remember anybody ever complaining about the change in the manner of exercising the salute.

It was exciting to move from Hawthorne School, where I had started Kindergarten in January of 1944, and completed sixth grade in January of 1951, to Leeds High School where I began seventh grade. Leeds really only had two schools, not counting the Catholic St. Michaels Elementary School, Hawthorne (grades K to 6) and Leeds High (grades 7-12). The move from grade to grade for me and my classmates was always exciting, but to go up the high school was really special.

In Kindergarten, I discovered on my first day in Miss Coffey's classroom, which was in the "garden level" or ½ story below ground level, that we were expected to take a nap. I actually had to bring a small rug to take a nap during the Kindergarten class time. For some reason, that seemed very difficult to me and I still have trouble napping during the day.

First grade introduced me to a new regimen. On my first day, Miss Ferris wrote a word in large letters on the chalkboard. The word was "DICK."[64] She said to the class, "I'll bet you don't know what this word is." I blurted out, "Yes I do – it's 'Dick.'" The teacher stopped, held up the palm of her hand and admonished me not to speak out in class without permission, embarrassing me in front of my whole class. I guess spontaneity in classroom discussions was perceived as some sort of threat, and that teachers could only allow students to express what they've learned if and when the teacher allows it. It sounded to me like a cat guarding the cream. Grudgingly, I and my classmates learned to live with the "heavy hand" of authority levied upon us for the next twelve years – sometimes equivocally.

In second grade during the war while Dad was away, we had to relocate to be near my maternal Grandma Flanagan Schultz. I was enrolled in Crescent Park Elementary School, located on the west side of Sioux City at the southeast corner of 27th Street and Myrtle – about 4 blocks from our home on 28th and George Streets. Moving back to Leeds in 1946 to Hawthorne School was like going home since most of my classmates hadn't changed much. Mrs. Pearl Manz was a delightful upbeat teacher, and she lamented with me that it took a couple of months for my spelling workbook to follow me back to Leeds from Crescent Park. We celebrated its arrival together.

---

[64] "Dick" was one of the main characters in the *Scott Foresman Reader,* which followed the life and times of the family of a young boy (Dick) and sister (Jane) and a baby sister (Sally). The family was typical for those days – mother was a stay at home housewife, father went to an office every day for work, the children had a dog, Spot, and the dialogues were amazingly simplistic, e.g., "See Spot run!" "Run, Spot, run!" etc.

Later on, Mrs. Manz interrupted a scuffle I was having with my brother, Mick, on the playground. She told us to stop, and my not-so-clever retort was, "It's OK, he's my brother." That did little to change her mind, so we had to settle down – for the better, I know now.

In fourth grade, a new immigrant — Norwegian student whose name I can't remember — joined our class, and he spoke not one word of English. Mrs. Teigen, our teacher, spoke Norwegian so the boy was placed in our class. We interacted with him daily, and he was fluent in English by the end of the year. Contrary to expert opinion, I've been convinced ever since that language immersion is one of the quickest ways to learn a new language. Mrs. Teigen (we called her Mrs. Tiger) was unpopular with me because she betrayed a promise once made to me. At Halloween time, I sported a black handle bar wax mustache, which cost me 5 cents. She confiscated it, put it in her desk and told me I could pick it up at the end of the year. I never forgot that worthless piece of wax, and on the last day of school I asked her for the moustache. She said she had thrown it away. That was a bitter lesson about adults — some people were not as good as their word. Amazing how a minor confrontation with disingenuousness shapes one's attitudes through life – and all over a 5¢ novelty.

Perhaps one of the best things that ever happened to me was a purchase that my folks made when I was about 10 or so. A door to door salesman came by one evening, and he was selling encyclopedias. Dad wasn't interested, but Mom was. Ever the avid reader, she thought the books would be good for me and my siblings. So they bought the *Richards' Topical Encyclopedia* on the installment plan. I loved those encyclopedias. I would sit and read them from cover to cover, and it was an illuminating and enthralling experience.

Richards Topical Encyclopedia – My Gateway to the World

I read about places in the world, scientific discoveries, famous people, and on and on. I remember that the Greek mythology section was interesting – especially the mythological Medusa with writhing snakes for hair. The range of my curiosity was boundless. Unquestionably, I learned much more from those books than I learned in classrooms.

There's little doubt that the development of my reading ability and interest was helped along with not only encyclopedias, but also comic books. Comic books were pictorial stories, and most of my interest in them focused on drama or superhero adventures. Crime fighting, heroic deeds, western adventures and helping mankind were the topics I enjoyed. My favorite titles included *Batman, Superman, Roy Rogers, Green Lantern, Prince Valiant, Tarzan, Dick Tracy, The Lone Ranger,* and others of similar kind. Once (or twice) read, they became commodities for trading.

When I had collected a number of the books and was ready for trading, I would get a box full and traipse over to a friend's house to begin trading. My friends with the best collections were Tom Galbreath and

Dale (Mick) McCuddin. They had excellent taste and they kept their comic books in good shape. We'd haggle over the trades in a friendly manner, and after reaching agreement, I would take my new found treasures home for more exciting adventures.

Recently I learned that some of those old comics had grown in value to hundreds and even thousands of dollars. That was good news. The bad news was that my folks threw all my comic books away when they moved out to McCook Lake in North Sioux City in 1959. Somewhere in a landfill in Northwest Iowa resides my moldering treasure of comic books – never to enrich my personal affluence. More's the pity.

Another incident, in sixth grade, lay in one piece of advice I received from Mrs. Landon, my elderly teacher, who told us that when we got to the high school, things were going to be different. For example, she explained, it was customary to stand up and ask the teacher a question or give a response if called upon. That advice eventually resulted in an embarrassing incident when I got to Leeds High School. In seventh grade in 1951, Miss Carter, an elderly spinster, called on me in English class. I stood up, and she looked startled, took a step back and said, "Where are you going? Sit down." I did so, and was flummoxed and became mute. She must have thought me dull witted or something, but I was embarrassed and thought my classmates would be sure that I was bonkers. So much for elementary school teacher's about high school decorum. Thus began my understanding of bumper stickers that advise, "Question Authority," and weakening my confidence in adult wisdom.

When I started 7th grade at Leeds High School in January, 1951, I had to walk considerably farther to Leeds High than I had to walk to Hawthorne. Hawthorne was on the northwest corner of 44th Street and Central Avenue, so it was little more than a block from my home up on the hill. Leeds High on the other hand was 12 city blocks away, or one mile. Walking in the cold weather was always unpleasant, at least until

I reached 16 years of age and obtained my driving license. I really don't remember it being cold, but I know it was because once I ice-skated all the way to school from home after an ice storm.

There was something very special about the teachers at Leeds High School. First, Leeds High School was small – about 200 students at most – so we knew everybody, including the teachers, many of whom lived in the community. I had learned the names of everyone behind me when I was a sixth grader, and then those ahead of me up to the 12th grade. I recall that most of the teachers worked after hours with students on extracurricular activities – plays, operettas, concerts, special programs, science fairs, etc. It was never difficult to get time with a teacher to get some extra help with the academics. Considering the compensation teachers received at the time,[65] their generous contributions of time, energy, and encouragement to students' developmental growth were way beyond what might have been expected. They certainly went the extra mile in our behalf.

One example of an excellent teacher was Mary Ellen Frakes , who was the best teacher I ever had – bar none. She had highly effective teaching skills that others didn't have. One thing I particularly enjoyed in her classes was that she capitalized on every minute we were in her classroom. She taught, "wall to wall" from the moment the bell rang to start the class. She was also the drama teacher, and directed many exciting and fun plays; including some where I had a part. She was also fond of using what are today called "sponge activities" to get classes

---

[65] In 1955 or 1956, the *Sioux City Journal-Tribune* published the salaries of teachers, presumably to embarrass them, but the salaries were so modest that most people I knew thought they were grossly underpaid. One salary stood out – that of Lowell Crippen, the head football coach – which was the princely sum of $7000 per year and the highest salary at our school. Can you imagine? I know from personal experience that Coach Crippen probably spent 10-12 hours a day at his job with football, basketball, track plus the math classes he taught on top of it all. I'm sure these dedicated exemplars have earned a special reward in Heaven for their selfless dedication.

started and on task with some immediate learning activity as soon as the bell rang. Her strongest skill was keeping us focused on learning, and actively engaged in meaningful tasks and challenges. Moreover, her positive personality and high energy always made her very enjoyable to be around and her classes to be captivating.

In ninth grade, Mrs. Frakes gave us an assignment to write our autobiography, which I found challenging, but effective in helping me master composition skills. I even made a wooden cover for it with the title of the essay burned into the wood. I named the autobiography, "Just Getting Started." Unfortunately, I lost that autobiography in a fire in 1983, but I guess this manuscript, over six decades later, could be named, "Wrapping it up."

Mary Ellen's husband was Bill Frakes, a US Navy veteran of World War II, who was also one of the teachers I truly liked and respected in Leeds High School (there were more than a few). Bill was responsible for teaching me the most useful and functional course in my high school education: typing! I took one semester of typing, learned the basics, and moved on not giving it much thought except when papers were required for courses. I used those skills extensively through my undergraduate college years and on through my five years of graduate school. Then about 25 years after high school graduation, along came personal computers, and from then on typing skills were not only useful, they were essential. They remain so today – including with this manuscript.

Mary Ellen directed several plays and operettas, the latter with Don Kelsey – a favorite teacher in music – and those thespian activities gave me several opportunities to handle appearances and performing before the public.

Our Miss Brooks (Comedy Play) January, 1957

*Left to Right: Me, Ron Burrus, Susie Rasmussen,
Dan Lundy, and Judy Jenkins*

The nice thing about a school like Leeds was that the social interaction with friends was always meaningful and rewarding. We all had opportunities to participate in activities that perhaps in larger schools would not have been available. It was also comfortable to know nearly everyone in the school, and to have a chance to work together on projects. Although my dramatic skills never manifested themselves in adulthood, I still had fun at Leeds High just taking a shot at something challenging – like acting before an audience. One of my favorite plays was "Father Knows Best" which involved several friends.

The Leader

Volume 31   LEEDS HIGH SCHOOL, Sioux City, Iowa   March 24, 1955   Number 4

Pictured from left to right are Judy Jenkins, Connie Clawson, Bill Poston, Tom Hooker, and Janice Harward. These five are known as the Anderson family in the all school play.

"Father Knows Best" Will be Given By All School Cast on Friday

March 25, this coming Friday, is a very important day at Leeds high school, for it is the day the all school play, "Father Knows Best," will be presented in the auditorium at 8 o'clock.

Fifty cents will admit all adults and the price for student tickets is 35 cents. Proceeds from the play will go to the student council.

"Father Knows Best" is a comedy in three acts about the Jim Anderson family and what happens when father decides to make the children stay home.

It all starts when he reads about two young people eloping, and from then on Father doesn't have anything but trouble from anyone.

Seventeen players make up the cast, which is directed by Mrs. Mary Ellen Frakes. Father, played by Bill Poston, is a youthful looking man in his early forties whose attempts to cope with family problems just don't work out. The mother, played by Judy Jenkins, is also in her early forties, but her attitude toward the family is more realistic than that of the father.

Janice Harward portrays their oldest daughter, Betty, a girl of 18, who combines her mother's good looks and her father's determination. Bud, played by Tom Hooker, is an athletically inclined boy of 15, who believes that girls are a pain in the neck.

(Con't. on Page 4)

Janice Harward Chosen As Candidate For FHA State Vice-President

Janice Harward, who is president of the Leeds chapter, has

Six Sociology Students Take United Nations Test

Six students from Miss Esther Groth's sociology class took a United Nations test on March 18, and the two best papers submitted by the students will be entered in the city contest.

Girls' Gym Teacher To Attend Convention

Attending a physical education convention March 29 to April 2 will be Leeds' gym teacher, Mrs. Hazel Klink. The meeting will be held at Lowry Hotel, St. Paul.

Leeds' Dean to Attend Chicago Dean's Convention

Leeds high's dean, Mrs. Alice Dawson, will attend a convention of the National Association of Dean of Women and Girls on Ap-

Father Knows Best – Another Comedy (1955)

Cast from Left to Right:
Judy Jenkins, Connie Clawson, Tom Hooker, and Janice Harward

In the picture above, the *Father Knows Best* cast included a group of friends with a modicum of talent, but not so much to get us on Broadway. Remember that we were a small school, I had many chances to express my (so-called) creative and active talents — participating in band, playing snare drum; orchestra, playing the whole percussion spectrum, including the tympani; vocal music, including choir, glee club, and the men's quartet; school newspaper, dramatics, performing in several plays and operettas; and athletics, including track and football.

Playing the drum in the LHS Pep Band (Mr. Sloan Directing)

I played tackle and linebacker marginally well enough to get me a football scholarship at Yankton College. Yankton was a division III School, probably hard up for members of their football team. However, it got me started on what would later total eight years of college.

Me at Left Tackle

It was an enjoyable sport in those days, but the violence and injury rates today make me think we were less brutal and truculent. It also looks like little fun and a lot of drudgery today – injury rates are off the charts. Regardless, looking at our team picture brings pangs of nostalgia – many of my teammates became friends for life.

LHS Football Playing Days, 1956[66]

---

[66] In the above team picture, I am No. 56 in the top row standing next to Bruce Yockey (no. 57).. My brother Mick is No. 11 in the second row. Dick Watt, No. 19, is on Mick's left and Bob Harward is in the middle of the second row, wearing No. 18, next to Jim Brehm, number 25. Al Hatler, No. 60, is in the back row, Don Johnson (back row) is No. 58, and in the third row is Larry Johnson,(no. 54), Joe Conley (No. 55), Dick Landers (No. 52), Tom Hooker (No. 51) and Joe Wagner (No. 22). Generally, any able-bodied male student who wanted to play football got to do so. We were all young and eager to play. Clark Hinesly is in the first row, (No. 15). Sadly, Clark died before graduation of acute Leukemia. Clark, a skilled tenor in my quartet, and a good friend, was a great loss to our school.

Our high school was small, which meant that special groups – football teams, band membership, etc. – eagerly competed for participants. One consequence of this was that when playing football, I had to run into the school building at halftime, take off my helmet and shoulder pads, put on my Band cap and cape, and run back out onto the field with my drum to play for half time.

Because there were only 13 in my class, we had the opportunity to sample a little of everything as far as student activities were concerned. No one has ever been able to convince me that small schools limit one's opportunities – most, if not all of us were involved in a plethora of activities. It was exciting.

Participation in extracurricular activities extended over sports, fine arts, and other special activities (newspaper, yearbook, science fairs, speech competitions, etc.). In the photo below, our music teacher, Don Kelsey, was a tremendous recruiter for vocal groups. I'm pretty sure that over 50 members of the student body were in the choir— this out of a student body of about 200 or so. I think Mr. Kelsey knew that widespread participation, regardless of talent, made for passable quality in delivering musical performances. There's a lesson there too – the more the merrier. Maybe that's because God wanted us to work together in unity.[67]

---

[67] On an aside, I learned from sociological research that groups are smarter and better at solving problems than any member of the group. That is, if individuals engage in solving a problem by themselves, the results they achieve are inferior to the results obtained by a group in which they are a member and solving problems. In other words, at least in problem solving, all of us are smarter than any of us, or the total is greater than the sum of the parts.

Singing in the Leeds High School Choir

(I'm the 5th one from the left in the
1st row with the light charcoal pants)[68]

My science teacher for all four years of high school was Charles P. Littlejohn. He was probably the spark for my interest in the sciences which I pursued later for my undergraduate degree. He taught all our high school science courses available to us at the time – general science, biology, chemistry, and physics. Remarkably, our physics class had only three students in it, but Mr. Littlejohn was still willing to teach it during his planning period. Bob Thews, Dan Lundy, and I were his sole, but apt students. "Charley" was a good guy who let me put my sack lunch in his classroom lab refrigerator, comprised of one pea-

---

[68] Given my lack of sartorial discernment, those charcoal pants were purchased upon the advice of my Aunt Karen (2 years my senior), who once called me aside at school to tell me that I needed to get some charcoal grey pants, a white turtleneck shirt, and white buck shoes if I was ever to make an impression on girls. I had the debonair outfit within a week.

nut butter and jelly sandwich, one bologna sandwich, a cookie, an apple, and a quart of milk that I brought from home. Sometimes, I was allowed to eat my lunch in the laboratory area at the back of his classroom.

Charles P. Littlejohn was a fascinating and clever man. He knew stuff, and I learned more from him that just about anybody, except for Mrs. Frakes. Charley, as we called him, said the same thing to every class I ever took from him except for physics, which was, "This is the worst class I've ever had." That was not some kind of motivator at work there. I think he was trying to shame us into behaving better, but actually the pejorative appellation became a badge of honor that we earned every year – the touch of irony was never lost on me. He also said about our lab times that "this is a <u>labor</u>atory, not a lab<u>oratory</u>." I loved that.

Mr. Littlejohn (he was always a mite formal) encouraged me in the 11th grade to create a science project and to compete in the Tri-State Siouxland Science Fair held at the University of South Dakota. My project involved building a carbon-arc furnace and electronically fusing carbon and silicon dioxide (sand) into an abrasive compound, silicon carbide. Later, on the commercial market it was called "carborundum." I never made a dime out of my inventiveness, but I did win first place in the event. It was exhilarating to be recognized so unexpectedly.

The size of our school also provided a wonderful form of personalized instruction. I greatly enjoyed science, and I had Mr. Littlejohn in science for four years in a row. Mr. Littlejohn was a gentle man, and I enjoyed being continually in one of his classes. All three of us went on in sciences, and Bob Thews later had a brilliant academic career in physics at the University of Arizona.

I had ample opportunity to develop some oratorical skills from many experiences including theatrical or dramatic activities like school plays and operettas, declamatory speech contests, etc. Many of those opportunities at Leeds High School have had a long and lasting influence on my life.

All A's: Janice Harward, Bob Thews, and I,
among others, are recognized

I would never claim that I was a sterling student, but with the close relationships among students and teachers, I demonstrated unusual achievement and felt good about doing well. A little recognition goes a long way – even affecting the eventual trajectory of my life.

For example, at graduation I was blessed to receive two scholarships – (1) Morningside College for academics (I was salutatorian – 2nd out of 13 in grades right behind Bob Thews, valedictorian) and (2) Yankton College for football. I eventually used both of those scholarships after my military service in 1957 – Yankton College's scholarship in football for my freshman year, and Morningside in academics the sophomore year.

*College Scholarship
From Yankton College[69]*

AL, Tuesday, August 13, 1957—3

Wins Scholarship

William K. ("Bull") Poston, jr., son of Mr. and Mrs. William K. Poston, sr., 4548 Central avenue, has received a scholarship to Yankton college, Yankton, S. D., and will enter as a freshmen in September. A graduate of Leeds high school, Bill was prominent there scholastically, in athletics and other extra curricular activities.

---

[69] (Note: My nickname was always 'Bill" – no one ever called me 'Bull" that I know of).

The Leeds High School Principal was Wiert G. Johnson (many students called him "Weird Johnson"). He was a stern and harsh disciplinarian, and seemed to relish intimidating students. I remember once, when Roger Cummings emerged from Mr. Johnson's office in an apparent bad mood. Donovon Rarick and I were walking toward the office in the boy's locker hallway, and Donovon said something innocuous to Roger. Roger suddenly turned toward Donovon and started smacking him – several times. Donovon wisely disengaged and quickly withdrew. We never knew what triggered the outburst, but my own supposition was that it was the result of an unpleasant experience with our dour and harsh principal.

I was once the recipient of Mr. Johnson's injudicious and grim demeanor for what he called, "defacement of public property." He called me into his office and in a most officious, overbearing manner read a statute from the Iowa Code about the penalty for "defacing public property," which was a $100 fine. In 1955, when this incident occurred, $100 was about what my Dad made pounding nails in a week's time. Johnson confronted me about writing my name on the 18" x 36" unpainted plywood panel above the stairwell leading downstairs to the band room, which was under the gymnasium-auditorium stage. I confessed to the transgression, but I had simply added my name on the panel alongside 40 or 50 other perpetrators, some of whom had already graduated or left school. The writing from others had been there a long time. My penalty for this transgression, delivered by Mr. Johnson in his most intense and condescending tone, was that I had to clean off the entire panel. Several sheets of sandpaper later the job was done, and I was released from further obligation. I steered clear of Mr. Johnson ever afterward. I also learned that brandishing your full name on public property wasn't very smart – most students, demonstrating greater skills than I, just used initials. This incident etched another verse on my scroll of definitions of acceptable behavior.

One delightful thing about education in Leeds was that when you reached the 7th grade, you knew just about everyone in the entire school system – six years behind and six years ahead of your grade level. That phenomenon has always made our occasional class reunions[70] much more fun that we would have normally expected.

Butterprint Plant – Noxious Weed in Iowa

Not everything of importance is learned in school. In fact, some of life's toughest lessons come from personal experience as we grow up. As an example, the fauna and flora of our area were a part of our activities outside of school. Despite some school lessons,[71] I wanted to give smoking a try. There is a weed in Iowa called "Butterprint" or "Velvet Leaf" that is very common in Iowa – especially in our area.

My brother and I decided to grind up some of it, roll it into a leaf and smoke it in Darrell Porsch's cornfield northeast of our house on Tyler Street. Both our parents were smokers, and of course when Mom and Dad did it, it only seems normal for us to try it too. Anyway, it was a disaster. We both got sicker than a dog, and vomited all the way home. To make matters worse, when we got home, Mick up-chucked in the kitchen – blowing

---

[70] Leeds High School class reunions are "whole school" reunions. Anyone graduating (or attending) from 1939 to 1972 may attend. They are usually every five years or so, thanks to Marlene (Bornholtz) Vanderloo, our unofficial student body president, who organizes and facilitates the events with élan.

[71] In school we were taught nothing about the health risks of smoking, but we were taught that smoking was an economic liability. In Mr. Norris's class, we learned that cigarettes cost 15¢ a pack, smoking one pack a day would cost something over $50 a year – which was an enormous sum for an 8th grader in 1952. That much money would have bought an old car in those days. Today, cigarettes cost over $5 a pack, and the annual cost is over $150 a month, which would easily handle the payments for a used car in good condition.

our cover. It didn't take long for Mom to figure out what had happened, but she didn't levy any punishment – I'm sure she saw that we had suffered enough already.

Humorous things frequently happened to me because of my gullibility and ingenuous inexperience. One example was while watching Grandpa Poston build a house in Leeds – I was about 10 years old – he asked me to go over to fellow builder Frank Knox's job site and borrow Frank's "board stretcher" so Gramps could use it. I pedaled my bike over to Tyler Street, found Frank, and told him what I needed. He told me to go back to Gramps and apologize because he had already loaned it to someone else. Truthfully, my gullibility kept me from realizing that no such thing exists, and that Grandpa was just having some fun with me. I loved his sense of humor. So much so, that I have been known to use some of his maxims and witticisms with my own grandchildren.

IX.

Integrity: Misdemeanors, misconduct and metamorphosis

"When reason fails, the devil helps!"
— Fyodor Dostoyevsky, Crime and Punishment

Misbehavior in Leeds was handled expeditiously, quickly, and persistently. Many years later, I learned in graduate school psychology courses that deterring criminal or iniquitous behavior involved the presence of two factors: proximity and certitude. Proximity refers to the time transpiring between the crime and the punishment. Proximity is an issue about the amount of time that elapses after a crime before accountability is imposed. Certitude is an issue if punishment is uncertain or is infrequently imposed. Without certitude, a perpetrator is likely to believe that it's easy to get away with the crime. If either of these conditions aren't met, punishment is less effective in shaping behavior. These factors – proximity and certitude – were always present in Leeds – things were handled swiftly and doggedly with accountability.

Certainly for me, crime never paid. One summer afternoon, my brother Mick[72] (2 years younger) and I were walking in the alley behind Harry Siedschlag's General Store. I was probably about 9 or 10 years old,

---

[72] Mick, born in 1940, regrettably passed away in 1997 of lung and liver cancer. Of course, his name was Michael but we always called him Mick (probably tagged on him by my Irish grandmother), until he was about 40 years old. Then inexplicably, he asked to be called "Mike." I teased him by saying that "Mick" was too ingrained in my DNA and it was impossible for me to make the change at that stage of my life. He got a big kick out of that, but he had a red cap that said, "Mikie" on it so I knew he was serious.

and Mick was 7 or 8. In the back of the store, through an open garage-type door, we spotted some cases with six packs of Coca-Cola in the 6-ounce green bottles. The temptation was great – we latched onto a six pack and took off running west down the alley. About 20 yards away, we heard Harry yell, "Hey – come back here!" We kept running and I told Mick not to look back so Harry wouldn't recognize us. This was definitely a bad plan. Leeds wasn't that big and everyone in town knew us — two tow-headed boys — what was I thinking?

We drank the Cokes in the park bushes surrounding the swimming pool north of 45th and Tyler Streets. When we got home about an hour later, my Dad met us at the door. "Where have you boys been?" he queried. "In the Park" I evasively said. "Did you go to "Leeds?"[73]

When my Dad started asking leading questions like that, I knew deep down in my soul that he knew what I didn't want him to know. At that point, I knew we were totally busted. With my eyes focused on the floor, I meekly said, "Yes." Then he asked what we did in the park, and shortly we began to cry and spilled the whole story. Well, we got a pretty good whipping over that. What was worse, we had to go down to Siedschlag's, apologize to Mr. Siedschlag, and pay for the Cokes <u>and</u> a deposit of 2¢ per bottle – these were 6 oz. green bottles with the "hourglass" shape. I still remember to this day that the Cokes were 25¢ for the six pack and 12¢ for the deposit. Of course, we had no money, so Dad advanced it to us and then we had to pay back the money with some onerous chores (mowing, cleaning the garage, and stuff like that). That was the most expensive 37¢ Coca-Cola I ever drank.

---

[73] We called the commercial area – three or four blocks of stores – "Leeds," so if you said "I'm going down/up/over to 'Leeds" you were saying you were going to the commercial zone of Floyd Avenue where all the stores were located south of our hilltop home about six blocks.

In any case, I believe that episode utterly convinced me that if I did something wrong; I was going to get caught. That feeling was bolstered by admonitions from my parents, which were frequent and often daunting. When our family would drive the 85 miles north to Sioux Falls to visit my five cousins,[74] we would occasionally pass the South Dakota State Prison in Sioux Falls. The prison sat high on a hill overlooking the entire city, and its high stone walls and concertina wire were foreboding and intimidating to all of us. I remember Dad saying things like, "if you don't behave yourself, that prison up there is where you will end up." Some exhortations never leave my memory bank, and that is one of them.

I never had much luck at any mischief I perpetrated not being discovered and disciplined. Once I took a cap gun to school – I was in the sixth grade at Hawthorne School at 44th Street and Central Avenue – and I showed it off on the playground. Somebody on the playground "ratted me out" as they say today, and I got wind of it. So I gave the cap gun to Richard Whitlock, step-son of Bill Siedschlag[75], to hide in his boot. He wore what were called "engineer boots[76]" and the gun fit in there nicely.

Once we returned to Miss Mabel Landon's sixth grade class, I was called out of the room by the principal, Mrs. Osborn – that was ru-

---

[74] My Dad's sister, Dorothy, was married to Clifford R. Clark, and together they had five sons – Gary, Gail, Randy, Melvin, and Cliff Jr (we called him Kip) – that we would visit from time to time on their farm west of Sioux Falls. The adventures we had roaming around the countryside with them could fill another book – one I might have called *My Experiences with a Civet Cat*.

[75] Richard was Bill Siedschlag's step-son and Harry Siedschlag's step-grandson (see narratives about Harry's delightful general store).

[76] Engineer boots were very popular with kids in Leeds – usually kids that were better off financially than most of us, since the boots were considered very expensive – around $15 a pair. Most shoes for boys were in the $6 to $10 range. By way of comparison, Converse (Chuck Taylor All Stars) tennis shoes which are still popular 60 years later and sell for $50 up, cost less than $10 in 1950. Note pictures of both types of shoes – however, my Converse shoes were black as most were in those days.

mored to have a rubber hose in her office for errant boys. She said, "Give me the gun you brought to school." I replied, "I don't have it." "Where is it?" she demanded. At that point, I didn't want to drag Richard down with me, so I lied, "I destroyed it and threw it away." Now in my experience, dishonesty always had unexpected consequences – nearly always detrimental to my well-being. Mrs. Osborn said then, "Okay, go get it."

*Engineer Boots c. 1950
(About $15)*

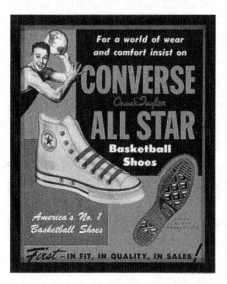

*Converse Tennis Shoes Ad
c. 1950 (About $10)*

I shot out of her office, ran nearly two blocks up the Central Avenue hill to my house, dashed in the back door, spurted up to my room, and grabbed an old cap gun. I then darted to the garage, grabbed one of Dad's hammers, smashed the gun, and stuffed the pieces in my pocket. I then flew by my amazed Mother, and ran as fast as I could back to the principal's office where I delivered the counterfeit evidence. Mrs. Osborn stared at me for a moment, and then picked up the phone, and dialed our home phone. She said, "Wilma (my Mom was the PTA President), I need you to come down to the school – we have a problem with Billy." I couldn't hear the other end of the conversation, but she said, "Thanks – I'll see you shortly." I was then directed to sit in a chair in the outer office outside Mrs. Osborn's office until my Mom came. In my mind, I was sure I would be beaten with that hose.

When Mom came, she went into Mrs. Osborn's office and closed the door. When she came out and gave me that "I don't believe you can be that stupid" look and said "Wait until your father gets home." That was the kiss of death in my mind. Dad was almost always the one to administer punishment, and he believed in the Old Testament justice of "spare the rod, and spoil the child." So for the rest of the day, I was brutally preoccupied with thoughts of doom because of my misconduct and considering how I might avoid a future of crime and punishment. In retrospect, I'm glad my "crimes" were of the misdemeanor variety.

Not that Leeds was a crime-ridden community. We had so little crime that no one locked much of anything. We never locked our car, nor did we ever lock our house. In fact, I don't think we ever had a key to the house. Both the front door and rear porch door had locksets, but no keys. Once, while down in Sioux City at Kresge's dime store, I bought a skeleton key for 5 cents and took it home to try it out. It worked. We put the key in the lock, turned it, and the door locked and then unlocked. I'm not sure what became of that key, but I know we didn't ever use it. Mom or Dad could lock the door with an inside latch. It was useful when they didn't want us in the house from time to time.

I remember Leeds as literally covered with a huge collection of trees. Oaks, maples, ashes, walnuts, and elm trees proliferated up and down and across town. There were some apple and pear trees here and there; including one in our back yard, but it didn't produce much fruit in the Loess clay bank east of the house. So, once, my brother Mick and I crept across Carlin Park behind our house over to Polk Street to steal some apples from a fully bearing tree of a neighbor. The owner came out and yelled at us and we took off across the park – thinking we had really pulled one off and gotten away with the crime of the year, until we realized that Mick had left his sneakers behind. Of course, the neighbor used a little detective work, and traced the shoes to us. Once again, our life of crime was nipped in the bud when Dad made us go back and apologize so Mick could get his shoes.

Now some things were too tempting to ignore. Some of these things were illegal but there were never any victims – like sneaking a swim in the Leeds Pool late at night. When I was about 15 on one hot summer night, Bob Harward and I were sleeping outdoors near our patio and garage, when we decided at about 11 o'clock p.m. to join up with Tom Hooker and go skinny dipping in the Leeds (Carlin Park) swimming pool, which was surrounded by a 6-foot high chain link fence. The pool was actually just off our back yard and down the hill about 75 yards or so. We crept into the park about 11 pm at night, took off our clothes and stashed them in some Bridal Wreath bushes, and scaled the fence. We were greatly enjoying the refreshing swim, when a police spotlight scanned the pool. We leaped out, naked as jaybirds and Bob and I climbed out over the fence on the side of the pool opposite the police. Tom decided to hide in a corner by the bath house.

Well, Bob and I made it back to our sleeping bags with our clothes, and pretended to be sleeping, knowing that the cops were still around somewhere. Pretty soon, my Dad shows up with a cop. He asked us if we had been swimming in the pool, and of course we confessed since we were pretty sure Tom had ratted us out and we were still soaking wet. He had been taken home to his mother (a very nice lady who I'm sure was very embarrassed about the incident). His punishment also included the embarrassing situation of being interviewed by the cops while standing there buck naked. The saving grace in this whole incident was that my Dad actually thought we had been pretty clever, gave me no whipping, just a tongue-lashing which was easier to take.

Sometimes, even when our misdeeds were unintentional, we still got nailed. On a cold, winter, snow-covered day, Tom Hooker and I – we were about 13 or 14 at the time — were walking down Central Avenue, shooting our BB guns at a tin can in front of us, when Mr. Spieker came running out of his house on the northeast corner of Central and 45th Street, and accused us of hitting his big insulated glass (Thermopane) picture window. We hadn't intended to do that, and neither of us thought we had. Evidently, an errant BB must have ricocheted off the frozen ground and hit his window. That little incident cost $50 and my Dad had to install a new Thermopane window in Mr. Spieker's house. It was just our luck to hit probably the only Thermopane window (dual glazed and vacuum sealed) that must have existed in all of Woodbury County at that time. A little cloud of bad fortune seemed to hover over my head at that point.

Speaking of deterrents, sometimes they are clear and understood, but feeble in enforcement. For example, I once spotted Jerry Calhoun (a big strapping, guy who was three or four years older than I was and who was playing football at Morningside College) wearing a white T-shirt one hot summer night that had an unusual inscription stenciled on the shirt. It said, "**3rd Team, Morningside Football.**" I thought to myself that would be embarrassing. Who wants to be known as a third stringer? Obviously, Jerry ignored the negative stencil. Didn't seem to bother Jerry, and I was not about to raise the issue with him because I knew he was on the first team. He was a gentle giant, but still a giant. I always wanted to stay on his good side for obvious reasons of survival.

Another incident demonstrating the effects of shoplifting occurred when I was about 7 or 8 years old. I was in the company with a neighbor at the S.S. Kresge's dime store in downtown Sioux City. A bunch of us were wandering around the store one evening – it was winter outside – and we wore our heavy coats. Eugene McPherson[77] had some Army Air Corps Surplus leather mittens that were sheepskin lined. We were heading out of the store, when this huge man grabbed all of us and sternly ordered us to accompany him to a windowless room at the back of the store. We were treated brusquely, and soon found out why this man was so hostile.

He took Eugene's mittens away from him, held them upside down over a table, and a little model car fell out with a clang. I had not observed how it got there, but all of a sudden we were all "criminals" and the man was calling our parents. All of us were questioned and our coats were searched, but poor Eugene was the sole recipient of his wrath. In about half an hour, we were released, admonished to go forth and sin no more, and severely chastised for Eugene's mishap and our aiding and abetting an alleged crime. I don't think I slept that night or the next, but the outcome served as a deterring effect on me all my life. I know that Eugene learned from the transgression, since I saw him at a high school reunion a few years ago, and he had led an exemplary life. I hope we all did.

A closing example of dabbling in the less than ethical and legal involved one of my classmates – Bill Owings, who for some reason decided to experiment in counterfeiting – an incident that further convinced both of us to keep on the straight and narrow. Bill, an extremely talented sketch artist, decided to draw the likeness of a dollar bill on a sheet of our school tablet paper. The tablets (mentioned earlier), 8½ x 11 inches in size, were provided by Sioux City Schools and were tinted with a faint tinge of green color. After cutting one page to size, Bill's dollar was so authentic that the lunchroom clerk down the

---

[77] Not his real name. The real guy knows that he made a stupid juvenile mistake – and I am not about to disclose his faux pas – especially since I saw him at a school reunion and we laughed over that experience, which scared us both straight.

stairs in the "garden level"[78] accepted it when Bill bought some chips and milk to go with his lunch.

After getting his change, Bill got cold feet, and rushed back downstairs to the "cafeteria" and purchased his bogus dollar back. Just seeing his sallow and ashen face before he recovered his illicit counterfeit money was enough to convince both of us that those shenanigans were not a good thing. Most of us have learned (usually the hard way) that crime does not pay, and it does deliver a fair modicum of guilt and abject fear to perpetrators. No fun that. Thank the Lord for conscience.

So, aside from eating an occasional watermelon snitched out of some Fairacres farmer's garden by some of my friends and me, my potential for a life of crime was stultified and quashed. Sixty years later, those lessons learned have never been forgotten.

---

[78] The "garden level" was actually the bottom floor of the school building, which was half below ground level and half above ground level, requiring the use of windows for illumination. Outside the windows below earth level were basement wells for egress. When there was a huge snow storm, the wells filled up with snow, making us feel like we were in an igloo.

X.

Exploration: Bikes, motorbikes, and automobiles

"Always focus on the front windshield and not the review mirror."
— *Colin Powell*

The bicycle was my main mode of transportation until reaching the ripe old age of 16, when I got my driver's license. Until then, getting around was either by "Shank's Mare," which is what my Dad called walking, or by bicycle. My first bike, when I was 11 or 12 years old, was a black, stripped down old 26" Schwinn that I bought from Neville Pelham[79] for $2. I used it a lot, but after a year or so, John Dreves told me that he thought my bike looked a lot like his old green one, which had been stolen. Of course, I never established the bike's origin, but I did note that Neville had bikes coming and going from time to time in his yard.

My most memorable bike was a 3-speed Indian (brand name) bike, made in Carlisle, Pennsylvania, which I purchased with my earnings from my paper route. That bicycle was my pride and joy – made me feel like I had a real Indian motorcycle. It was unique in Leeds, since it was a beautiful shade of dark red, had narrow tires, a 3 speed shift, a luggage carrier on the back fender, and a tire pump. I loved the low gear it had for when I had to peddle up the 46th Street hill on Central Avenue on my way home. It made delivering newspapers a breeze.

---

[79] Not his real name.

Indian Bicycle (c. 1951) My $40 Pride and Joy

The bike did a couple of things for me. First, I learned that if I worked at something and accepted responsibility, I could better my life substantially. I also learned that achievement of an economic asset through my own initiative was better than having it given to me. For example, after I bought my own bike, I was somewhat envious that my brother and sister were given bikes by Mom and Dad, since I had saved up and purchased my own bike. Ironically, their bikes became temporarily unavailable to them when they were repossessed by the Lone Star Hardware store in Sioux City because my Dad had failed to maintain the payment schedule. Two burly guys showed up with a truck, and took Mick and Lynda's bikes away. The bikes came back after the payments were caught up to date. I never had that problem since my purchases were usually cash from my own resources. In retrospect, my brother's and sister's experiences seemed to me to be an irregular journey of dependence upon others, frequently from Mom and Dad for money and things. I learned that it was better to rely on myself financially, even though it seemed grossly unfair at the time. Gratefully, my own children have grown up to have the same independence and determination.

In any case, the Sioux City Journal-Tribune (afternoon daily) and the Des Moines Sunday Register (Sunday only) were my main sources of income in those years and gave me modest purchasing power. Other odd jobs, lawn mowing, baling hay, shoveling snow, etc. helped as well.

MIGRATING TO MOTORIZED MOVEMENT

Most of us need a motorized vehicle to get us where we need to go for means of employment and income, and I was no exception. For many years before I was able to drive, I imagined what it would be like to have all that power in my hands. Unfortunately, my aspirations for driving far exceeded the actuality of learning how to do it.

First, my Dad and Granddad were in the construction business, and my Dad's work vehicle was a 1936 Chevrolet pickup, red in color with black teardrop fenders and a narrow truck bed. That is the vehicle in which I learned to drive, starting about 1951, when I was about 13.

Learning how to drive was a home-based operation. Dad's old pickup is what he and Mom used to teach me to drive. Since we lived on a dirt road, we simply drove west toward Fairacres on 46th Street until we got to what is now called Rustin Street and drove on the country roads north of there. Those narrow dirt roads had fearsome deep ditches on both sides. It was tricky to stay centered just right, but a thrill to hold the wheel and press the gas pedal.

1936 Chevy Pickup Truck (Four on the Floor the Hard Way)

My first actual driving experience was when Mom let me drive Dad's truck from Floyd Avenue six blocks north to our house on Central Avenue after school. When I drove by Dick Watt's house, he and his brother Tom were out in the front yard, so I yelled out the window to them and waved. That was my first mistake. When I diverted my eyes from the road, the vehicle began veering in that direction too. Mom's shriek brought me back to attention to the road, and I narrowly missed the curb. It was a long while before she let me behind the wheel again.

For months afterward, whenever I got a chance, I practiced with that old Chevy truck on the dirt roads north and west of Leeds. It was harder to drive then than it is today, since it was a floor-mounted transmission, manual with four forward gears and one reverse gear, and it required considerable dexterity and coordination with a manual clutch in order to shift gears and not jerk or stall the vehicle.

When I turned 14, it was legal in those days to drive a motor bike. I saved up the money — $40 from my paper routes and odd jobs, and bought a Whizzer motor bike. It was great to ride – in good weather of course – and cheap to maintain. It only went about 25 or 30 miles an hour, and got 50 miles per gallon mileage.

Whizzer Motorbike (c. 1952)

Once I was riding my Whizzer southwest on Floyd Avenue near the Leeds Library when a car headed northeast turned left onto 41st Street, and hit me broadside. I flew through the air and ended up on the library steps. Fortunately, I wasn't hurt beyond a few bumps and bruises, and the bike was damaged but not too seriously. The driver didn't even stop, so I never knew who it was or whether or not it was unintentional.

Another time, I was headed north toward Leeds past Albertson's tool factory on Floyd Avenue when an oncoming car started to pass a southbound car, entering my lane. That time I swerved to the side of the road to avoid being hit, but tumbled into the weeds between the road and the Floyd River near Springdale.

People in cars often have their eyes so fixated on their route, they do not see motorbikes or motorcycles. It's as if the cycles are not even there! Ask any motorcycle rider and they will tell you how truly scary that really is. I learned to drive the Whizzer defensively after that.

Once I reached the "accountability" age of 16, and finally got my driver's license, Dad would let me drive one of his newer trucks, like his shiny green 1954 Ford F-100 pickup.

1954 Ford F100 Pickup (My Luxury Limousine on Dates)

That truck was great on dates, but somewhat humbling at the same time. On the doors, emblazoned in silver trimmed in red was the company name for all to see:

C. H. Poston & Son
Building and Remodeling
9-9727 or 9-3022

Signage on Dad's 1954 Ford Pickup Doors

Needless to say, it was hard to maintain anonymity or much privacy with such a message on the side of the truck. That logo just cried out, "*HEY! If you see me doing something stupid in this truck, just call one of these numbers and tattle on me!!!*" No question that I was motivated to be circumspect while driving that truck. Like many small towns, if I did something stupid while driving around Leeds, I couldn't get home faster than my Dad would hear about it.

That fear never seemed to bother my brother, Mick. Once, I was driving Mom homeward up Central Avenue, and we saw our family car, a 1951 Chevy blue and white sedan, driving northward ahead of us a couple of blocks. Mom wondered if Dad had gotten home early, which absolutely never happened that I can remember. When we got home, and the car was in the garage and no driver was to be seen. We went in the house, and found Mick in the kitchen. Dad wasn't home. Mick denied driving the car (he was only 14 years old), but the stack of tarps on the driver's seat provided contradictory evidence. He was caught – twice – once for taking the car and then lying about it. Mendacity was a huge no-no for my dad, who administered the usual punishment with his belt, which even I felt badly about. I'm sure not as badly as Mick felt, but I had been there often enough myself to sympathize.

After a while, I rounded up enough money doing odd jobs, and I purchased my first car – a 1940 Chevrolet that I picked up for $100. It was nothing to brag about but it was <u>mine!</u> It was a 2-door sedan, black in color, and had a six cylinder engine. To spiff it up, I put on an exhaust extension so people would think I had dual exhausts. Actually it was a "Y" that connected to the tail pipe after the muffler with flexible piping extending to both sides of the vehicle. If it hadn't been for that car's lame suspension system that held the back end of the car up about 6 inches higher than the front end, I might have gotten away with the deception. As it was, I removed it after some heavy ribbing from friends.

It's truly hard to believe, but I could drive that junker down to Wixon's Conoco on the corner across from Wilkins' Drug on Floyd Avenue and Tyler Street, buy a dollar's worth of gas and get <u>5 gallons!</u> In May of 2012, in Lahaina, Maui, I paid $5 and got 1 gallon of gas! Gasoline was cheaper in my youth – no doubt about it – even when you calculate the time value of the 20¢ per gallon to today.[80]

Of course, I still had lessons to learn with my "new" Chevy. Showing off for my buddies, we drove southwest on Floyd Avenue to 21st Street, west on 21st to Court Street, south on Court Street to Gordon Drive, and then west to Riverside Avenue and then north to "Stevens," crossing into South Dakota (now called North Sioux City, South Dakota). It was a great joy ride, and we were headed for Elk Point (about 22 miles away, where Don and Larry Johnson's grandparents lived), when all of a sudden the motor seemed to explode. It made a terrible clanking noise, and we stopped by the side of the road in Jefferson, about 15 miles from Leeds. Fear of what had happened hit me in the pit of the stomach, but even more fear clutched my innards when I realized

---

[80] The real price of a 20¢ gallon of gas in 2014 was $3.39, indicating that something other than inflation has been at work.

the excruciating part was yet to come. I had to call Dad.

By then it was about 7 pm at night, and I told him what had happened. He said he would come get me, but he asked, "Where are you?" I feared it might involve my premature demise, but I told him. Naturally, he blew his stack and wanted to know "what the hell" I was doing in Jefferson. I had no good explanation. He came out to get us, hauled us back to Leeds, and scolded me all the way home in front of my friends. It was a long ride home and another painful lesson. Eventually Dad had it towed to one of his buddies, who worked on it in his spare time in his home garage. It cost $40 to rebuild the engine, which of course, I had to pay.

1940 Chevrolet 2-Door Sedan Like My First Car

My first automobile accident occurred in 1954, when I tangled with Dad's new Ford F-100 pickup. That 1954 pickup was Dad's pride and joy, and he kept that truck immaculately clean (as he did with all of his tools or equipment). Unfortunately for me, he parked that truck behind my car about 20 feet away, which in a moment of haste I forgot. I jumped in my car, started it up, and threw it into reverse and stepped on the gas. All of a sudden, I crashed into the front of his truck, scaring the blazes out of me. I jumped out and surveyed the damage. My car suffered the worst of it, but my rear bumper was under his front bumper. Dad came out and saw what had happened, and he headed for the garage to get a 10-pound sledge hammer all the while issuing a stream of choice profane comments. The trunk of my car was never the same after he dislodged it from his pickup with brute force.

Later, I acquired a 1948 Chevy sedan, much more "luxurious" and mechanically sound but also well used and cheap. In 1956, I was driving up Central Avenue, heading home, when at 44th Street, Audra Cole shot out from the west, and drove her 1946 Ford convertible right out in front of me. There was a terrific collision as I "T-boned" her car. Thankfully no one was hurt, but my pride was wounded seriously. The 1948 Chevy was not worth fixing after that, so we cannibalized it for parts, and sent it to the junk yard where we got $15 for it.

So I started my life-time voyage with automobiles progressing through better cars in terms of quality but with correspondingly higher costs. The voyage continues to this day, but memories of my old, durable, and initial Chevy's still endure – especially now since cars have extended in cost beyond what people used to pay for an elegant three bedroom home in the Sioux City Country Club area.

XI.

Epilogue: Surprises, ideas, and adventures, mistakes, lessons learned

"Try not to become a man of success. Rather become a man of value."
— *Albert Einstein*

As in any undertaking like a chronicle of one's life, I can't avoid reflecting upon my experiences, what I learned, and what I have become. I believe I have grown in wisdom, which I've heard is characterized by the ability to make sensible decisions and judgments based on personal knowledge and experience – often gained by learning from bad decisions and judgments.

There has been no shortage of poor decisions and judgments on my part over the years, but I have learned from each and every one of them. Sartre was quoted as saying, "We struggle with all our strength all of our lives against the crushing view that our mistakes control our destiny." In my own life, there has definitely been a connection and I don't grapple with it or resist it. It wasn't so much my mistakes, but my inferences from the "hard knocks" of real life.

Youth passes, but love is forever

Family has always been a very critical part of my life. I was born into one that taught me many good things along with some things I vowed never to replicate. When I became old enough I started my own family, and when my time comes I will leave one behind. Lessons learned from parents and grandparents stay with us throughout our time on this planet. Marriage has always been forever in my and my wife's family tree, and "till death do us part" was never compromised. We've continued that legacy and tradition faithfully

I pray and hope that my legacy will be a family that comes after and emulates loving God and loving our neighbors. Love is what matters.

Hard work is its own reward

One lesson I carried away from my youth was gained when I worked construction with my Dad and Granddad. They taught me the <u>real</u> meaning of work. I wonder if that knowledge gained might be more typical of my generation, since I worked alongside two earlier generations and that introduced me to their trials, travails, and tribulations that they endured without complaint well into their golden years. Their continually arduous, difficult, and exhausting labor, in the misery of working outdoors in bitter cold or scorching heat, convinced me that construction for me would probably have been a mistake. My destiny lay elsewhere — in more academic pursuits and human services. Not for the less demanding physical aspects, but for the intriguing and exciting world of human interactions, endeavor, and opportunities for service to others.

My 1957 Leeds High Lancer (Yearbook) Graduation Picture

People are more important than things

Long after leaving Leeds, my family and I experienced a devastating fire in 1983. We lost everything – clothes, furniture, appliances, tools, family heirlooms, pictures and memorabilia extending back to our own childhood. Despite the loss, I found comfort in a verse from the Bible that came to me about not storing up treasures on this earth. I of course grieved the loss of my stuff; especially things my Granddad had given me from the Civil War – letters, pictures, etc. – that he had gotten from his Grandmother, after his Grandfather (my Great-Great Grandfather Fielden Poston) had died in the war. But I had to let all my stuff go and move on. My family was all safe and sound, and we survived. This value has been with me for my entire life, and guides my thinking on things like wage theft (I think it needs to be outlawed and punished), minimum wages (low wages actually exacerbate the need for government welfare and family support), and universally accessible and affordable health care. Don't try to convince me that the richest country on the planet can't afford to provide that for its citizens.

Honesty is the best policy

I'm sure that I fibbed and equivocated as much as anyone as a youth, but as an adult I learned that telling untruths could damage one's reputation, undermine integrity, and produce serious feelings of guilt. Telling a lie to my Dad was nearly a mortal sin. He would really blow up over that, and when he was angry, it was best to hide in the park behind our house. I can only think of one time later in life when telling a lie was constructive, and that was when our neighbor's dog ate my daughters' pet bunny rabbit that used to run in our back yard. The cage had been ripped open, and the bunny was gone. My 7-year old daughter asked if the bunny had escaped back into the wild, and I answered, "That's one possibility." I just couldn't hurt our young daughter's feelings, or make her resentful of the neighbor's dog. Compassion motivated me, but it still was dishonest and I set it straight many years later. I found later in my chosen profession of public leadership that disingenuous statements were a death knell for credibility and career, so I have always tried to shoot straight.

God is bigger than we know

In my years in Leeds, I constantly marveled at the beauty of my environment, and its place within the entire world. Sitting out in our yard after dark and admiring the night sky always made me feel humble. Learning about the speed of light and the distance to even the closest star, gave, and continues to give me a perspective of my insignificant place in the universe. Fifty years later, I'm still learning about "laws[81]" and the mysteries of nature and feeling awe and reverence at the immensity of the universe. It's impossible for me to put God in a box given the unbelievable magnitude of the universe – now some 13,783,000,000 years old. Moreover, the intricacies and carefully executed phenomena of our planet in my mind can only be the result of monumental planning and design. My God is a BIG God. Nevertheless, a key precept, learned decades ago, continues to motivate me: It's not enough to show my faith without works, but it's most important to show my faith <u>by</u> my works.[82] Words alone don't cut it – actions speak much louder and authenticate faith.

If it's to be, it's up to me

My youth convinced me that if I were to succeed in life, I had to do it myself, because no one was going to hand it to me on a silver platter. I

---

[81] "Laws" of nature are in effect ways and means that our limited intellectual abilities describe phenomena we see recurring or occurring in the world and universe around us. There are many unexplainable phenomena (i.e., black holes, dark matter, and an expanding universe) that perplex me, but I am not so arrogant as to assume that I should be in charge of it all. I just submit to God's omnipotence with awe and wonder.

[82] *James 2:18*

avoid dodging responsibility or trying to shift responsibility to someone else. For example, I raised money to buy my own bike at age 12 or so, but my siblings had theirs provided by my parents. I continued on assuming responsibility for myself, and met my needs more than adequately, including working my way through college. It's easy to blame the world for one's circumstances, but it's far more constructive and pragmatic to just take things on with a resolve to succeed in accomplishing realistic goals without external dependencies. Of course, prayer helps as well.

Do it right the first time

My years of working off and on for my Dad and Granddad provided me with numerous opportunities to try things for the first time. My Dad always stressed that taking shortcuts was a sure way to do a job inadequately. He used to say, "Do it right or do it over." I did many things over, and learned that there was a right way and a wrong way to do things. Usually, the way that was most tempting, because it was quicker or easier or sometimes cheaper, turned out to be the wrong way and did require starting over – taking longer in the end. Gramps and Dad modeled the old adage for me, "There are no shortcuts in life, only those we dream up." This precept is a part of me – sometimes I am sue it's in my DNA.

Be ready to drive nails when the bell rings

This is another message imbedded in my being from my Dad. He was always an early riser – I mean really early – like no later than 5:30 am. His idea was that if work is to start at 8, then we had to be on the job no later than a full half hour before that. That gave us time to unload the tools, sort out the materials, and have everything ready to "drive nails" when the bell rang at 8 o'clock sharp. At the other end of the day, quitting time was not the "exit" time, but it was the time when we stopped driving nails and then started buttoning up, cleaning up, loading tools and materials, etc. In other words, a full day's work was a full eight hours. I find it hard after six decades to even consider being late to an appointment or a function. I am not comfortable unless I arrive early and when the time comes, to be fully ready to undertake the activity. My perspective is that if I arrive for a job early, I'm on time – if I arrive on time, I'm late. It may be a compulsion, but believe me, it works.

Self-importance is a painkiller for stupidity.

I shared earlier about what my Mother frequently said to me when I was on a jag of self-aggrandizement, that "You're no better than anyone else – you're just as good, but no better." And sometimes she would add, "And don't you forget it." That ethic is as strong in my bones today as it was when she said that to me. I will always champion the underprivileged, the vulnerable, and poor until the day I die. Others disagree with me, but I firmly stand on the equality of people before their creator, and that "except for God's grace, there I may go too." Everyone in this land – the richest country in the world – should have equal access to health care, opposition to which makes no sense to me whatsoever. People of all backgrounds and origins need to be treated justly, fairly, and equally under the law, but I know that sometimes equal isn't fair or righteous. Fairness may require unequal help or assistance due to different levels and criticality of need. Some folks have handicaps or other disadvantages due to circumstances beyond their control and therefore need more help than others – in other words, equity.[83] I value that all people, regardless of personal or hereditary characteristics, stand equally before God, so who am I to challenge his omniscience?

---

[83] Equity is variable help or assistance in accordance with individual needs. One size does not fit all.

United we stand and well, you know the rest

Early on and all through my youth, I learned about team participation. The Roberts Dairy Pop Warner team, the Leeds High School Band, my membership on many teams, running the *Leeds* Leader school newspaper, participating in the cast of plays and musicals, and working in many other groups are only a few of the legion of experiences that emphasize the point that united we stand or divided we fall. Our country's motto is E Pluribus Unum (from many, we are one). I also remember from Sunday school that "The body is a unit, though it is made up of many parts; and though all its parts are many, they form one body."[84] And the point is if anyone in the body is hurting, everyone is hurting. If anyone wins, everyone wins. Loving your neighbor isn't just a slogan, it's a commandment.

I also learned that any group is smarter than the sum of its members. In my later professional life, I placed groups into problem solving situations. The individuals were to work on the problem provided and come up with alternatives to deal with the problem. Their solutions were graded, but not disclosed. Then the same people got into groups of 5-7, and dealt with the same problem, which was also graded. Ironically, and surprisingly to everyone involved, the group scores were always higher than the scores of any member of the group. I concluded, that "all of us are smarter than any of us." Groups are smarter, more productive, and superior in problem solving than any member of the group. Someone once asked me why that was so, and I hem-hawed around and finally said, "I don't know, but maybe God wanted it that way – so we would work together." That was good enough for me then, and it is good enough for me now.

---

[84] *Corinthians* 12:26

You never walk alone

In Don Kelsey's choir class, one of the more enjoyable songs we fre-quently sang was "You'll Never Walk Alone," by Rodgers and Hammer-stein from a Broadway play presented in 1945. The popular recording of our day was a rendition of the song by the Fred Waring Chorus (that Don was once a part of), and the song was featured in the 1956 movie, *Carousel,* with Shirley Jones and Gordon MacRae. It was a great film to share with a date. We sang the song many times in our choir classes, and the words still reverberate in my mind:

> When you walk through a storm, keep your chin up high
> And don't be afraid of the dark. At the end of the storm
> Is a golden sky and the sweet silver song of a lark.
> Walk on through the wind, walk on through the rain
> Tho' your dreams be tossed and blown. Walk on, walk on
> With hope in your heart and you'll never walk alone....
> You'll never walk alone.[85]

The lyrics were always powerfully meaningful, the music delightfully melodious, and the song never failed to lift my spirits whenever trou-bles or tribulation came along. Of course, the meaning was never lost on me – the poetry of the words is an allegory for the Holy Spirit, which many times in my life gave me hope, solace, and reassurance that it's always okay to not be in control of life's episodes and to trust God with my destiny.

---

[85] *"You'll Never Walk Alone (original version 1945)". YouTube. Retrieved April 20, 2011* (Rodgers, R. and Hammerstein, O. You'll Never Walk Alone. *Carousel* (Musical). New York. 1945).

THE PAST IS PROLOGUE

This book was a labor of love for me. I have so many amazing recollections and memories of growing up in Leeds that seemed to visualize an enchanted place in my mind that I just couldn't selfishly keep to myself. After many years of reflections and reminiscences, I decided to create a manuscript that shares insights into my youth up to and through high school, capturing all the nostalgia I could muster. Despite moving on and acquiring three college degrees, and achieving a modicum of social and economic success, I have never felt far from the multitude of experiences that brought me to adulthood and now full maturity with well over seven decades accomplished and precious few, if any, to go. The story ends at my high school graduation, but the things you find in this discourse make up who I am and how I got there.

My Family on My Graduation Day, January 20, 1957

(Left to Right: Brother Mick, Mom, Me, Sister Lynda, and Dad)

As I write this only my sister has survived with me to this point in time. Both Grandmothers and Grandfathers, my Dad, my Mom, and brother Mick are all gone, but I carry many memories and remnants of their times in my heart. Of course I miss them, but deep down they are a real part of me. They helped mold the stuff of which I am constituted, and I am grateful for their influence on my life. Other than my sister, an aunt, two uncles, and a number of cousins, the attrition of my family has continued to progress. I do take comfort in the fact that I am now at the ultimate end of a familial chain – giving now to my children and grandchildren after receiving from my parents and grandparents.

Wednesday, January 20, 1957, I graduated with honors as class Salutatorian. Not the top, but close to it, and the valedictory would have been mine except for Bob Thews who skipped a semester and graduated early. I'm OK with that. Remember what I said about self-aggrandizement? Besides, the salutatorian of a group of only twelve classmates isn't like conquering Mount Everest or solving world poverty. I just felt good about completing an important milestone. Graduating from high school was a big deal back then. It was a significant achievement and one which I looked upon with great satisfaction and sense of accomplishment.

So one door in my life closed, and another opened. At my graduation, much lay ahead for me in the several decades of my life yet to come: a rich and comprehensive education; a Godly and loving wife, Marcia, for well over five decades; two wonderful daughters – Heather Boeschen and Holly Kaptain — who remain very close with their equally wonderful husbands – Tim and David, respectively. And most especially our six amazing and delightful grandchildren that have blessed us immeasurably – the three Kaptains: Alex, Elea, William, and the three Boeschens: Abby Kate, Grant, and Maggie.

In 1957 at age 18, I had no idea that ahead for me waited a magnificent career in education, many honors and distinctions, astonishing experiences all over the world, eighteen published books, prosperity and the most important aspect of life – a wonderful and loving family. God is so good.

And – you can yell it.

Acknowledgements

(You Can Yell It: Coming of Age in Leeds, Iowa)

It was if it had been predestined – there we all were – in Sioux City, Iowa, attending the first Leeds High All-School alumni reunion in July, 1986, almost 30 years after graduation. The gathering had an excitement that was palpable as everyone plunged in around food and libations to get reacquainted, share tales of our lives, and to remember the fun and momentous times as we grew up and came of age in small town Leeds, Iowa.[86] The energy of the two day reunion was exciting – we would laugh at one recollection and cry at the next. At the end of the 48 hour chaotic joy, it became apparent to me that what we had loved and lived in Leeds needed to be captured and collected as stories in a book, with a genuine narrative framed around our alliance of friends who grew up in Leeds – what we experienced, how it was immeasurably unique, what we learned, and how it impacted our adult lives.

The epicenter of much of my school years orbited around a club that was named the "BDB's" by its three pre-teen members. Many years later, the club, although not a secret or formal organization, had special meaning to the three of us, who bonded together for fun and exploration of the world in and around Leeds, from elementary school to high school graduation. During our auspicious assemblage, consisting of Bob Harward, Dick Watt, and me — Bill Poston — we played out about a fifteen-year agenda that included learning, swimming, playing, climbing, running, exploring, and riding bikes and later cars all over the Leeds community and often beyond.

---

[86] Leeds, Iowa was platted April 15, 1889 on 154 acres three miles outside the city limits of Sioux City but was annexed to Sioux City October 20, 1890, following a referendum.

Our club gathered an overabundance of adventures, journeys, escapades and shenanigans with an occasional smidgen of mischief. Our informal relationship flourished for over a decade, up to and including college, even sharing membership in the Sigma Phi Epsilon fraternity at Morningside College, after which we dispersed, with Dick remaining in Iowa, Bob locating in Colorado and Oklahoma, and Bill locating out west in California, Arizona, and Montana. For three decades, we had contact with one another only occasionally, but the BDB bonds remained strongly viable across the miles and through the years.

Fortuitously, Marlene Bornholtz Vanderloo a fellow alumna (and gifted cheerleader) of our small school, sparked a movement in 1986 to invite everyone who ever attended Leeds High (the school had closed in 1972) to attend a gathering of all Leeds High School Alumni. Her hard work and selfless endeavors brought graduates and former students of LHS, including the BDB's, together at the Marina Inn Conference Center in South Sioux City, which provided a great setting for our "BDB Club" to socialize, reminisce, remember, and reflect on the experiences of the "three BDB's" in Leeds. For years afterward, BDBs' occasional get-togethers, interactions and additional Leeds High reunions delivered a fertile assortment of treasured memories that I started jotting down on a list. My plan eventually was to pull the experiences together in a volume of memories to describe what it was like to come of age in the 1940's and 1950's – exhilarating and wonderful years to be young in rural America – when I could give it the time needed. All I needed was content from my friends and family, a unifying thematic approach, and time to put it together. That time has arrived, and what you hold in your hands is the compiled rendition of myriad captured memories – precious to me and I hope heartwarming and enjoyable to anyone who picks it up and visualizes how Leeds made us what we became. It was a journey back in time, and it was a wonderful trip into a magnificent and memorable era for me.

Appreciation is due to many who helped with this herculean task, and

I am immensely grateful to the following:

- First and foremost, I am grateful for the love and encourage-ment afforded me for the past 54-plus years in all my work and writing endeavors from my wife Marcia. She has been my faith-ful and devoted helpmate, with whom my life has been won-derfully rich and meaningful well beyond what I deserve.
- Next, as an author and a parent, I cherish the love and support of my family – Heather and Tim Boeschen, and Holly and David Kaptain, and their respective families. Thanks to them, Marcia and I have also been graced with six marvelous and brilliant grandchildren, who have given me enthusiasm to document and record what it was like to come of age in Leeds in the mid-20th century. Mainly, this book is for them.
- I would be remiss not to mention that I'm especially blessed with Heather and Holly's intellectual critiques and Heather's indispensable proofreading skills. They make my scribbling look good.
- I also must thank the best man for my 1961 wedding, and my fellow BDB, Bob Harward, to whom I owe a special debt as my favorite source and sounding board of stories and legends of our youth. We shared a plethora of experiences and activities in Leeds, and it is still exhilarating when we get together and laugh and cry over the many things we shared as kids. Of course, we both miss but fondly remember Dick Watt, the 'D' in BDB, whom we lost in 2001.
- Finally, I dedicate this book to my six incredible grandchildren – Kaptains: Alex, Elea, and William; and Boeschens: Abby Kate, Grant, and Maggie – for providing me with great joy every day and for the inspiration to create this testimony of my youth and how it made me what I am today. I pray they enjoy it.

The memories contained herein are as accurate and complete as I can remember them – any errors or omissions of course are mine. I hope you enjoyed reading about coming of age in Leeds as much as I enjoyed putting *You Can Yell It!* together.

William K. Poston Jr.

December, 2015

Bibliography of Images and References

Image or Reference
Photo or Quotation Source
(Sequenced by Order in Manuscript)

Image: Leeds High School 1939-1972
Photo in: F. Gaskell, M McArthur, D. Gordon, C. Lydon, and C. Gaskell. (1991) *A pictorial history: 1889-1989, 100 Years, Leeds, Iowa.* Sioux City, IA: Leeds Community Club. P. 106

Image: Sioux City Postcard
Owned and furnished by author

Image: Leeds Castle, Kent, England
Retreived from Wikipedia,
https://commons.wikimedia.org/wiki/File:Leeds_Castle_-Kent_-England-3July2007-102.jpg 18Aug2015

Reference: prices in 1938
[1] Adapted from http://www.answers.com/Q/What_did_things_cost_in_1938.

Image: Floyd Avenue 1911 in Leeds
Owned and furnished by author (postcard celebrating Leeds centennial 1989)

Image: Leeds Main Street 1952
F. Gaskell, M McArthur, D. Gordon, C. Lydon, and C. Gaskell. (1991) *A pictorial history: 1889-1989, 100 Years, Leeds, Iowa.* Sioux City, IA: Leeds Community Club. P. 137

Image: Al Hatler Haircut
Photo in: *Leeds High Lancer.* Leeds High School Yearbook. Volume XI, 1957. P. 70
Owned and furnished by author

Image: Siedschlag Advertisement
Football Game Program Excerpt, Leeds High School v. Spencer High School. September 15, 1956

Image: Leeds Carnegie Library
Retrieved from University of Iowa website, http://clip.grad.uiowa.edu/sioux-city-public-library-leeds-branch 31Aug2015

Image: Aerial view of Leeds
Retrieved from Google Earth, https://www.google.com/maps/@42.54786,-96.36125,1194m/data=!3m1!1e3 Imagery c. 2014 Google, Map data c.2015 Google (Courtesy of Google, Inc.)

Image: Leeds Variety Bowling Team
Retrieved from Facebook, https://www.facebook.com/LeedsIaUsa/photos 7 August 2015

Image or Reference
Photo or Quotation Source
(Sequenced by Order in Manuscript)

Image: S&H Green Stamps
Owned and furnished by author

Image: Bill with Lucky 1949
Owned and furnished by author

Image: Bill and Mick in Dad's first Boat
Owned and furnished by author

Image: Fairacres Swimming Hole
Owned and furnished by author (photo taken July, 2011)

Image: Intrepid Skinny Dippers
Courtesy of SuperStock, © 2015 SuperStock (4186-15976). Used with permission.

Image: Iowa Snapping turtle
Owned and furnished by author

Image: Boy's Swimming at the YMCA
Retrieved from Yahoo! Images,
https://sp.yimg.com/ib/th?id=JN.KekTyDC3z3pPyl7Y91jllA&pid=15.1&P=0&w=300&h=300, May 21, 2015

Image: Keith Wixson's Conoco
Leeds Conoco Station. Courtesy of the Sioux City Public Museum, Sioux City, Iowa.

Image: Great Northern Moving Fast
F. Gaskell, M McArthur, D. Gordon, C. Lydon, and C. Gaskell. (1991) A pictorial history: 1889-1989, 100 Years, Leeds, Iowa. Sioux City, IA: Leeds Community Club. P. 139

Image: Chicago and Northwestern Caboose
Retrieved from Wikipedia,
http://en.academic.ru/pictures/enwiki/67/C_%26_NW_RR_Caboose_12432.jpg, May 19, 2015

Image: Charles Floyd Monument
Owned and furnished by author

Image: Leeds – Illinois Central Depot 1950
F. Gaskell, M McArthur, D. Gordon, C. Lydon, and C. Gaskell. (1991) *A pictorial history: 1889-1989, 100 Years, Leeds, Iowa.* Sioux City, IA: Leeds Community Club. P. 8

Image: Streetcar at Wilkins Drug
Original photo taken by Grover Wilkins c. 1946 (deceased), F. Gaskell, M McArthur, D. Gordon, C. Lydon, and C. Gaskell. (1991) A pictorial history: 1889-1989, 100 Years, Leeds, Iowa. Sioux City, IA: Leeds Community Club. P. 123

Image: Leeds Graduating Class January 1957
Photo in: *Leeds High Lancer.* Leeds High School Yearbook. Volume XI, 1957. P. 70

Image or Reference

Photo or Quotation Source

(Sequenced by Order in Manuscript)

Image: Speeding Car Hits Tree, 2 Die

Courtesy of: *Sioux City Sunday Journal*, October 27, 1957. Vol 38, No. 28, p. 1.

Image: Cherry Bing Candy Bar

Photo retrieved from,

http://www.palmercandy.com/assets/caches/images/assets/uploads/general/101
00_twin_bing_1.875_good_count_bar3-500x335.png, 2 November 2015

Image: Skid (Steer) Loader

Retrieved from, http://s7d2.scene7.com/is/image/Caterpillar/C10552268?$cc-s$
16 October 2014

Image: Austrian Pine

Retrieved from,

http://twinspringsnursery.com/sitebuilder/images/Vanderwolf_08-112x150.jpg 13
February 2015

Image: Author at 18 months

Owned and furnished by author.

Image: Author at 3 years

Owned and furnished by author.

Image: Horse drawn drag scraper

Retrieved from http://amhistory.si.edu/onthemove/collection/object_175.html

Image: Council Oak and cars (Flood 1953)

F. Gaskell, M McArthur, D. Gordon, C. Lydon, and C. Gaskell. (1991) A pictorial history: 1889-1989, 100 Years, Leeds, Iowa. Sioux City, IA: Leeds Community Club.
P. 130

Image: Leeds Residents evacuating by boat (Flood 1953)

F. Gaskell, M McArthur, D. Gordon, C. Lydon, and C. Gaskell. (1991) A pictorial history: 1889-1989, 100 Years, Leeds, Iowa. Sioux City, IA: Leeds Community Club.
P. 131.

Image: Poston Polk Street home under water 1953

Owned and furnished by author

Image: 1953 Flood Cleanup

Flood Cleanup Photo. Courtesy of the Sioux City Public Museum, Sioux City, Iowa.

Image: Snow hits Siouxland

Retrieved from http://www.ktiv.com/story/27773752/2015/01/06/photos-snow-
hits-siouxland May 23, 2015

Image: Killer snow storm in NW Iowa

Owned and furnished by author

Image or Reference
Photo or Quotation Source
(Sequenced by Order in Manuscript)

Image: Scooting along on an American Flyer sled
  Kids on a sled, Retrieved from
  http://historyinphotos.blogspot.com/2012/05/marion-post-wolcott-kids.html May
  23, 2015

Image: Poston Family during WWII 1945
  Owned and furnished by author

Image: Ken and Wilma Poston in California 1943
  Owned and furnished by author

Reference: Screen Shot
  Found in *Victory in the Pacific 1944-1945*. Disc 3: Reader's Digest WWII in the Pacific. Questar, Chicago, IL. (2010).

Image: Ken Poston in Saipan, July 1944
  Isaacs, J. (Producer), & Frankland, N. (Director). (1969). *World at War* [DVD]. United Kingdom: Thames Television. Viewed on U.S. Military History Channel (September 5, 2012).

Image: Poston children, 1947
  Poston family photo, Lacey, S., Artist, charcoal rendering of family photo. Owned
  and furnished by author.

Image: Pot-Bellied Stove
  Pot bellied stove, retrieved from
  http://www.northerntool.com/shop/tools/product_2053_2053 Item# 172892. 2
  November 2015

Image: Kitty Clover Potato Chip Tin
  Vintage potato chip container. Retrieved from
  https://www.pinterest.com/pin/54606214205174255/ May 21, 2015

Image: John Leo Schultz 1910
  Owned and furnished by author

Image: Cathryn Irene Flanagan 1911
  Owned and furnished by author

Reference: National Register of Historical Places
  Retrieved from: http://www.siouxcityhistory.org/historic-sites/131-woodbury-
  county-courthouses

Image: Woodbury County Courthouse 1918
  Family postcard owned and furnished by author

Image: Cathryn Irene (Flanagan) Schultz 1975
  Owned and furnished by author

Image or Reference
Photo or Quotation Source
(Sequenced by Order in Manuscript)

Image: Mom and Dad at 25th Anniversary 1963
Owned and furnished by author
Image: Gram and Gramps 1965
Owned and furnished by author
Image: LHS Girls Basketball 1953
Leeds High School photo, retrieved from
https://www.facebook.com/LeedsIaUsa/photos/ September 14, 2015
Image: LHS Leader April 1955
Leeds High Leader. April 6, 1955 (Volume 31)
Image: Grolier's Book of Knowledge 1952
Vintage encyclopedias, Retrieved from http://www.amazon.com/Complete-1952-Book-Knowledge-School-Subject/dp/B003U7NSHM March 18, 2015
Image: I Speak for Democracy
Excerpt from *Leeds High Leader,* Owned and furnished by author
Image: Homecoming Court 1956
1956 Homecoming photos. Retrieved from
https://www.facebook.com/LeedsIaUsa/photos/ March 18, 2015
Reference: C.S. Lewis
(Footnote) Retrieved from:
http://www.cslewisinstitute.org/Christianity_Makes_Sense_of_the_World
Image: Drum & Bugle Corps on 4th St in Sioux City 1952
Owned and furnished by author
Image: Hawthorne Elementary School 1891-2010
Hawthorne Elementary School photo, Retrieved from
https://www.facebook.com/LeedsIaUsa/photos/ March 18, 2015
Image: Poston and Harward Kids 1946
Owned and furnished by author
Image: Poston Kids En Route to Wisconsin, 1948
Owned and furnished by author
Image: Mick and Bob, Sons of American Legion 1951
Owned and furnished by author
Image: American Legion Parade in Des Moines, IA 1951
Parade article, *Des Moines Register.* August 8, 1951. P. 3
Image: Richards Topical Encyclopedia
Family photo. Wright, E.; Wright M; Richards, j. (1945) *Richards Topical Encyclopedia.* New York: J.A. Richards Publishing Co.

Image or Reference
Photo or Quotation Source
(Sequenced by Order in Manuscript)

Image: Our Miss Brooks
 Leeds High School Lancer.(1957) p. 53. Owned and furnished by author.
Image: Father Knows Best
 Leeds High Leader, March 24, 1955, p. 1. Owned and furnished by author.
Image: LHS Pep Band
 Leeds High School Lancer.(1957) p. 70. Owned and furnished by author.
Image: LHS Football Days, 1956 Left Tackle
 Leeds High School Lancer.(1957) p. 31. Owned and furnished by author.
Image: LHS Football Team
 Leeds High School Lancer.(1957) p. 30. Owned and furnished by author.
Image: LHS Choir
 Owned and furnished by author
Image: LHS Leader article – BP got all A's
 Leeds High School Leader, May 1956, p. 1. Owned and furnished by author.
Image: Bill's Scholarship Article
 Sioux City Journal, August 13, 1957.
Image: Butterprint Weed
 Iowa Butterprint photo. Retrieved from
 http://iowaweedcommissioners.org/butterprint-abutilon-theophrasti/ May 21,
 2015
Image: Engineer Boots
 Popular boot in 1955. Retrieved from http://vintageengineerboots.blogspot.com.
 March 18, 2015
Image: Converse Tennis shoes
 Popular shoes in 1955. Retrieved from http://legendaryauctions.com. March 18,
 2015
Image: Carlisle Indian Bicycle – 3 speed
 Bike photo. Retrieved from Theclassicbicycleshop.com March 18, 2015
Image: 1936 Chevrolet Truck
 Owned and furnished by author
Image: Whizzer Motorbike
 On display in the Sugar Bowl Ice Cream Company, Decorah, Iowa. Photo courtesy
 of Heather Boeschen, 2013.

Image or Reference
Photo or Quotation Source
(Sequenced by Order in Manuscript)

Image: 1954 Ford F-100
Pickup photo, Retrieved from http://www.barrett-jackson.com/Archive/Event/Item/1954-FORD-F-100-PICKUP-130958 November 2, 2015.

Image: Signage on Dad's 1954 Ford F100 Pickup
Original art: Owned and furnished by author

Image: 1940 Chevy
1940 Chevrolet sedan. Retrieved from http://3.bp.blogspot.com/1940Chevy_SymphonyLake_800pix.jpg. March 18, 2015

Image: Bill's 1957 *Lancer* picture & caption
Graduation Photo and Information. Leeds High School *Lancer* (Yearbook). P. 8.

Image: My Family on Graduation Day 20Jan1957
Owned and furnished by author.

Reference: Song Lyrics
Retrieved from: *"You'll Never Walk Alone (original version 1945)"*. YouTube. Re-trieved April 20, 2011

(Rodgers, R. and Hammerstein, O. You'll Never Walk Alone. *Carousel* (Musical). New York. 1945).

About the Author

Dr. William K. Poston Jr., better known as Bill, was born on Armistice Day in November, 1938 at St. Joseph's Hospital, 21st and Court Streets, in Sioux City, Iowa. He grew up in Leeds, graduating from Leeds High School in January, 1957. Dr. Poston earned his BA degree in sciences at Iowa State Teachers College in 1961, now the University of Northern Iowa. His Specialist and Doctoral degrees were earned at Arizona State University in 1966 and 1968, respectively. Bill began his educational career as a math and science teacher in 1961 and later served 25 years in educational administration positions, including a secondary principalship in Mesa, Arizona, and 15 years as a superintendent in three school systems in Tucson and Phoenix, Arizona, and in Billings, Montana.

In 1989, Bill and his family returned to Iowa where he served at Drake University as a professor of school finance and business management, and in 1990 moving to Iowa State University in Ames, Iowa, where he now holds the position of Emeritus Professor of Educational Leadership and Policy Studies. He retired from Iowa State University after serving for 15 years, and currently resides in Johnston, Iowa.

Bill's military service spanned 14 years. He served in the Iowa Air National Guard from 1955 to 1958, and served in the United States Marine Corps Reserve from 1958 to 1961. From 1964 to 1972, he served as an artillery battery commander in the Arizona Army National Guard.

Dr. Poston has received many professional distinctions, including service as the youngest-elected international president of the distinguished educational society, Phi Delta Kappa International, and in 1980, he received a national "Outstanding Young Leader in American Education" award. During his professional career, Bill has authored or co-authored dozens of professional articles and 18 books in educational leadership and financial management. *You Can Yell It!* is his first historical autobiography.

Bill has been married for over 54 years to Marcia Bottorff Poston, whom he met at Iowa State Teachers College. They have two daughters, Heather Boeschen (husband Tim) and Holly Kaptain (husband David). Six grandchildren bless and complete the family – Alex, 21; Elea, 19; and William Kaptain, 17; and Abby Kate, 15; Grant, 13; and Maggie Boeschen. 10. All three families live close together in the northwest area of Des Moines, Iowa, where they enjoy life in America's heartland.

Books by the Author

1. *Teaching Indian Pupils (*Center for Educational Advancement, Mesa, AZ, 1966*).*
2. *An analysis of teacher morale and community attitude.* (Thesis, Education – Specialist. Arizona State University, 1966).
3. *Predicting School Administrator Success.* (Doctoral Dissertation, Arizona State University, 1968).
4. *The Most Significant Educational Research Contributions of the Last Ten Years. (*Co-author) Phi Delta Kappa Center for Evaluation, Development, and Research. 1974).
5. *Making Schools Work: Practical Management of School Operations* (Corwin Press, 1992).
6. *Effective School Board Governance* (Center for Educational Research. Phi Delta Kappa International, 1994),
7. *Making Governance Work: Total Quality Education for School Boards,* (Corwin Press, 1994).
8. *Generally Accepted Audit Principles in Curriculum Management* (with F. English, Acme Press, 1999).
9. *The Curriculum Management Audit: Improving School Quality* (Co-author, Scarecrow Publishing, 2002).
10. *The Three Minute Classroom Walkthrough: Changing School Supervisory Practice, One Teacher at a Time.* (Co-Author, Corwin Press, 2004).
11. *The Sage handbook of educational leadership: advances in theory, research, and practice (Contributing Author) Sage* Publications, 2005).
12. *The Three*-Minute Classroom Walkthrough (Co-Author) (Multimedia kit for professional development. Corwin Press, 2006).
13. *50 Ways to Close the Achievement Gap* (Co-Author, Corwin Press, 2009)
14. *50 Ways to Close the Achievement Gap: Multimedia Kit for Pro-*

fessional Development. (Co-Author) (Corwin Press, 2009).

15. *Advancing the Three Minute Walk Through: Mastering Reflective Practice.* (Co-Author Corwin Press, 2010.)

16. *School Budgeting in Hard Times: Confronting Cutbacks and Critics.* (Corwin Press, 2011).

17. *Handbook of Educational Leadership: Second Edition.* (Contributing Author. Sage Publications, 2011).

18. *The Sage Guide to Educational Leadership and Management.* (Contributing Author. Sage Publications, 2015).

19. *You Can Yell It!: Coming of Age In Leeds, Iowa.* (Historical Memoir. Outskirts Press, 2016).

Index of Individuals

There are many, many people in Leeds, especially students and faculty of Leeds High School that need to be in this book. All who interacted with me in Leeds merit recognition in a book like this, and they deserve an expression of thanks for the support, kindness, and courtesy afforded me. Regrettably, not all were able to be included in the narrative and I offer my sincere apologies for any who may have been omitted – unintentionally.

189

CPSIA information can be obtained
at www.ICGtesting.com
Printed in the USA
FSOW04n1416180216
17102FS